I0145370

THE COMING OF THE GUARDIANS

AN INTERPRETATION OF THE "FLYING SAUCERS"
AS GIVEN FROM
THE OTHER SIDE OF LIFE

COMPILED BY

MEADE LAYNE

FORMER NATIONAL DIRECTOR OF
THE BORDERLAND SCIENCES RESEARCH ASSOCIATES

INNER CIRCLE PRESS
San Diego, California

This edition published
1956
by The Inner Circle Press
San Diego, California
by special arrangement with
Borderland Sciences Research Associates

New material, revisions and cover
© 2009
Inner Circle Press
All rights reserved

ISBN 978-1-58509-525-4

Cover layout
by
Toni Villalas

Published by
The Book Tree
P O Box 16476
San Diego, CA 92176
www.thebooktree.com
We provide fascinating and educational products to help awaken the public to new ideas and
information that would not be available otherwise.
Call 1 (800) 700-8733 for our *FREE BOOK TREE CATALOG*.

INTRODUCTION

After more than half a century this book was found in the archives of the Inner Circle Foundation, the home of Mark Probert's amazing body of publications and audio presentations. Meade Layne and Probert were residents of San Diego and were very close. They shared information and research for many years, with this book being just one example of the pioneering results they achieved. For a time, Borderland Research was located on Adams Avenue in San Diego, just a block away from the current Inner Circle headquarters. Probert was the greatest psychic medium of his time, much forgotten today, but was famous for his channeled teachings from various unseen, intelligent sources. Much of the information received solidly backed Meade Layne's pioneering UFO research.

Where do UFOs really come from? Layne holds an interdimensional, etheric-based theory. He terms those from the other realms as "Etherians" and the UFOs themselves sometimes appear as living creatures, referred to as "aeroforms." Much of the information was corroborated by the scientific work of Trevor James Constable or came directly from the intelligences channeled through Probert. Layne was scientific in his approach until hearing Probert's amazing messages, which independently verifies his research. This book covers propulsion systems, vibrational frequencies, and the sudden appearance of these craft more accurately than most scientific books on this subject have ever done.

Paul Tice

CONTENTS

This book is dedicated to those metaphysicians of
the Western World who, as yet, have not enlarged
their frame of speculation beyond the boundaries
of things corporeal. It deals with the problem
of the Aeroforms, or Unidentified Flying Objects,
and concerns their nature, origin, and the reasons for their incursion at this historically
climactic juncture.

The separation of Science from Metaphysics and Oc-
cultism is arbitrary, and this must be recognized
if the problem is to be understood. This applies
also to the existence of the ether(s) and the
principle of emergence. The Communicators here
quoted are excarnate humans, but what they say is
without philosophical bias and untainted by relig-
ionism.

All that the compiler of this book can hope for, is
that it may reach some readers sufficiently receptive to scan its pages without prejudice and try to
consider the problem as a whole. Future years will
add much to its content, but the basic interpretation will neither be contradicted nor impaired.

THE COMING OF THE GUARDIANS

- F O R E W O R D -

In this Foreword we shall try to be as concise as possible, on a subject of such complexity, and do little more than state the present situation, the basic ideas involved, the reasons why many people find it difficult to accept these, and the sources of the information offered in the main part of the text. The situation in brief is simply that the whole of our modern civilization is confronted with certain disquieting and inexplicable happenings, involving both a great danger and a great hope - and that there is little in our contemporary culture, in science or religion or philosophy, which enables us to think about these facts intelligently, or even accept them as objective and as of crucial importance.

The incursion of the Aeroforms and the Space People began its present phase some eight years ago - though similar events are now believed to have occurred more than once in centuries past. Perhaps some future historian (if any) will devote a volume to a Brief History of Human Stupidity in the 20th Century, and select these eight or ten years as the incredible high-water mark of his subject. There is no need to detail the ignorance, the puerility, the pseudo-scientific flubdub, the cackling silliness of the press and radio, and the bigotry and incompetence of authorities. The record is in millions of words of print and nauseating to reflect upon. This phase of attempted preparation on the part of the Guardians is fast nearing its close, and has been, on the whole, a failure. A rough guess might be that out of 160 million people in the United States, less than a million accept the existence of the "saucers" and other aeroforms as factual and objective. And it is not likely that a tenth of these are mentally prepared for the events which are probably impending. Apart from a pitiful handful there has been no one to prepare them - and all the accumulated stupidities of our century conspire to bog them down.

The same reasons which result in this 'bog-down' of the human intelligence will obviously hinder the present acceptance of this booklet, and they may be summarized somewhat as follows: (1) There are metaphysical and philosophical ideas involved in any real understanding of the Aeroforms, and the Western mind is strongly preconditioned against importing such ideas into what is called 'science' - even though speculative science and mathematics always end in metaphysics unless arbitrarily delimited. (2) The purely scientific ideas and concepts touched on in these pages have no text-book status and are regarded as too speculative for serious consideration (by technical science, at least). (3) The explanations of the Aeroforms and other phenomena given here, are sanctioned and expounded by excarnate human beings, who can and do communicate with here-living people in various ways - as well as by etheric beings themselves, who are not excarnate humans. This, of course, raises a huge question-mark in the minds of millions of the prejudiced and uninformed.

Nothing can be done for or with people of that type, at least not in any prompt and urgent way; thus the contents of these pages will profit them nothing. (4) The so-called etheric or "4-D" explanation will be regarded with hostility by orthodox religionists, and very dubiously even by most Western occultists - who perhaps should know better but do not. One of the most appalling aspects of this whole cultural impasse is the near-hopeless inadequacy of occult knowledge in both East and West, about facts of such immense importance. (5) Finally, the visitation of the aeroforms and all that it implies demands an effort to think in new terms, in new ways about new facts, and a rejection of old and cherished ideas, than which nothing is more repugnant to the average human mind.

Those of us who have given a near-decade of study to the Aeroforms and their related phenomena, are well aware that a sizable handful of people throughout the world have correct basic information, some of whom hold positions of high authority in civil government, in the armed services, and in the world of science. These people know, they are deeply apprehensive, but nearly helpless in the face of problems of such character and magnitude.

This brings us to another obvious remark, that everything in this booklet can be no more than a sketch and outline of the planetary situation. Out of a thousand possible questions, two or three are answered - yet these two or three are basic, vital, and of primary importance. Also implied are several good reasons why, unless you are unusually receptive and well informed, you should not read these pages, or talk too much about them if you do, nor try to overturn any more of the already alarmed hives of orthodoxy, in science, government, and religion.*

About the communications quoted in the following pages, here I shall say only, that the "etheric" or "4-D" explanation was first announced in the fall of 1946 - and that all the data accumulated since then can be logically subsumed under it - that no later data contradict it - and that no other explanation as yet has been offered anywhere which is in any way adequate, nor in fact worth the paper it is written on when it attempts to cover all aspects of the phenomena. Nor have the Controls (the Communicators) ever retracted or basically altered any statements as first given by them - though these have been expanded by application to new happenings. What you are about to read are stenographic and tape recordings of deep trance mediumship, given through the non-professional medium Mark Probert, now widely known for his

*Note: At the time of this third printing (May, 1956) the etheric interpretation is receiving much favorable attention, especially among the English investigators. Comments in the United States also show increasing interest and approval. ML

remarkable gifts. These communications have been under intensive study for some eight years past, and we have found our invisible friends to be learned and honorable persons, and in every way well disposed and anxious to help.

To those who regard it as sheer effrontery, to present an explanation of the Aeroforms given by those on 'the other side of life', we have only one request to make: Will you not disregard the alleged sources of the information and consider the material on its own merits, as science and as metaphysics, and as the only explanation offered which 'saves' all phases of the phenomena. What do you care whence it comes, IF it answers your questions rationally and with reasonable completeness? Or, try to say something rational and intelligible yourself - remembering that many millions of people accept "transcendental" communications as often valid and authentic.

There are also those who say: 'We believe in survival and communication - and there are thousands of 'seances' held every night in the year. Why was not the whole matter cleared up long ago?' Without depreciating the psychic contributions of spiritism, this is too important a question to be handled with over-nice diplomacy. The average excarnate human knows nothing of the etheric worlds. He does not linger in them after death, was taught nothing about them here, and enters and dwells in the vibratory rates of astral worlds and substance. The universe swarms with life in every part, and each of us goes to his own place by his own physical-and-mental 'gravitational' compulsion, as truly as iron sinks or cork floats or gas rises. A few humans do enter the etheric regions at times, through some karmic conditions (as may be the case with some of the Rolf Telano Communicators.) We are told that the Etherians die on their own plane, and usually reincarnate there after a very short time. Let us always remember, in trying to explain and understand these phenomena of the Visitation, that they are enormously complex, complex as the universe itself, that there is no simplified explanation possible, and for our thinking there are only hints and clues and 'lines of probability'. No, 'spirit communication' in the broad and usual sense has not been helpful during these last eight years of puzzles and complexities. And the great occult Orders, as previously hinted, have hardly been in better case so far as any worthwhile pronouncement is concerned. But the Mark Probert Controls, at least the 16 or more who compose the "Inner Circle", have long shown themselves to be persons of a very high level of intelligence. They have personally studied various aspects of the Etheric worlds and have access to them - which is possible, like all other things, to those who have persistent will and desire. Here and there, of course, there are others of similar caliber, both on our plane and on astral and etheric levels, who also have the knowledge and desire to serve humanity. To them, as to the Mark Probert Controls, we acknowledge a great and unpayable debt.

Perhaps this is the best place to remind our readers that what is reported here is in the nature of informal conversation - not lectures or scientific essays or treatises. The same ideas are restated from different angles, and some expressions at first glance seem contradictory, but these will usually clear up with a little reflection. And the lack of any scientific training and vocabulary on the part of the intermediary (Mark Probert) makes it difficult for the Controls to be precise and accurate. Such matters will be easily understood by readers familiar with psychism and mediumship generally. It seems advisable, also, to take a few pages more for a summary of the Etheric Explanation, or "4-D" theory, to facilitate understanding of the talk of the Controls.

The Etheric or   The Aeroforms (flying discs, etc.) are for the
"4-D" Explanation   most part EMERGENTS; that is, they emerge onto our
of the Aeroforms: plane of perception from a space-time frame of reference which is different from our own. This process can also be described as a conversion of energy and a change of vibratory rate. When this change is effected, the disc or saucer becomes visible and tangible. It appears to be, and IS what we call solid substance, until the energy rate is reconverted. It amounts to a process of materialization and dematerialization (mat and demat). Energy is forever changing its forms. Invisible steam becomes visible vapor, the vapor becomes a liquid and the liquid becomes a solid (ice). This solid "dematerializes" under a blast of heat. Electricity, the 'flow' of invisible electrons, can be produced by radiant energy, but it appears to our senses as light, heat, color, sound, and motion. There are colors we cannot see (below the red and above the violet), and sounds we cannot hear. We live in a sea of waves, radiations, emanations, vibrations, but our senses can respond directly to only a few of these, our instruments to only a few more. All this is the commonplace of science - and has been known equally well to metaphysical and occult thought for thousands of years.

Just as there is a spectrum of sound and color, there is also a spectrum of tangibility. This is a little more difficult to understand. What one might call the upper end of this spectrum is familiar enough; vapors, gases, the air itself, radiations of all kinds cannot be detected by touch. Any solid can be vaporized, and so disappear from our perception. But the important point here is, that matter can also be too dense to be touched. What we call solid matter is really a wide-open mesh, with immense distances between the 'particles' within the atoms - as every schoolboy knows. Lead is supposed to be a very dense metal, but a cubic inch of it (say) could in theory be compressed to pin-point size, and beyond that to invisibility, and there would still be plenty of 'room' between the atoms and the parts of them. This lead particle would then be invisible and untouchable - and would pass through other substances, such as wood or cork or steel, as easily as a rifle bullet through the air. It is easy to see that there may be (and indeed there are) material worlds - worlds of dense substance all about us, which we are unable to touch because they are too dense, not too rarefied. And some of these objects may at times be touchable but still invisible (colors we cannot see) and make all kinds of sounds which we can't hear.

These worlds can interpenetrate with ours, and in turn be interpenetrat-
ed by others of still higher density, and our normal senses would never
report any of them. If the Aeroforms are to be understood in their true
nature, as Emergents, it is essential that those elementary ideas be
clear in our minds.

This extremely dense matter of the invisible worlds equates with the
Ethers, and also with Space. Space is not nothingness. "Empty space"
is not even an idea, but merely a vocal sound to replace thinking. It
is probable that there is an "infinite" series of ethers, i.e., of vibratory rates of extremely dense substance* - and this substance responds
to the play of the finer forces, including the "energy"** of mind or
thought. Any shape can be thought into existence in etheric matter,
and if its vibration rate can then be lowered to the right point (de-
crease of density) the shape or object can be seen and touched on our
plane. If the vibratory rate is increased again, the object will disappear. If we were to vaporize and then recondense a brick, keeping the
vapor-form within the same original volume, the operation would be an
analogous one.

The importance of this matter of density, to our present inquiry,
stems largely from the repeated assertion by the Controls, that the
Discs "come out of worlds of substance a hundred thousand times more
dense than the matter you perceive by your senses." We cannot defend or
explore here the concepts involved in such a statement, but we shall
have to get some glimpse of them if we are to have even the most remote
understanding of the true nature of the aeroforms. Our remarks about
density so far may have seemed very naive to the physicist, and it may
be useful to quote briefly from the mathematician, Lindy Millard:

"In scientific literature -- i.e., technical journals -- more than
one kind of density is mentioned. The terms most frequently used are
electron density (number of electrons per unit volume) and energy density, besides the mass density. The meaning of grain density seems
self-evident. Vibration density, though seldom mentioned as such, can
be expressed by associating together in a common region two other kinds
of density: a high grain density with a low mass density.

"All discussions in which the word density is used should specify
what kind of density is meant. Is it mass density, or grain density, or
some other such as energy density or power density. Power being the
same as work divided by the time during which the work is done, it
would seem that power density may in some instances mean work multi-
plied by the frequency density, and in some other instances, energy-
density per vibrational cycle period. . . ."

*Bertrand Russell defines an electron as "a wave of probability with
nothing to wave in". **"Energy" of mind in quotes because it does not
conform to the physics-definition; does not obey the "law of inverse
squares."

Lindy Millard, by reasoning from electrical analogues, has also made a rigorous mathematical rerivation of the following generalized basic formula for the ether itself where optical waves are being propagated.

$$\text{Frequency at resonance} = \frac{V \underline{\hspace{3cm}}}{\text{PRESSURE}}$$

$$\text{Square root of pressure over}$$

$$\text{K x sq. root of mass density} \qquad \frac{K \times V \underline{\hspace{2cm}}}{\text{MASS-DENSITY}}$$

where K is a constant that may depend on the material substance saturated with the ether..Frequency depends on the inverse square root of mass-density of the ether itself.

Relativists who feel convinced that the concept of the ether has been abandoned and wholly displaced by the contemporary mathematical approach, should examine the studies of R. Wussow, C. F. Krafft, and Hermann Fricke.

One of the communicators quoted, the Yada di Shi'ite, gives us a very helpful illustration. Consider, he says, a nest of ten balls all free to move within each other, such as are often carved out by oriental craftsmen. For any point on, say, the inside of the outermost ball, there will be a corresponding point on its outside, and on the outside and inside of the second ball, and of the third and so on, through all the ten concentric spheres. Any object on any sphere can emerge at its corresponding point on any other; and since there is no "empty space" to be crossed, but the massive continuity of the ethers fills everything, the 'crossing' will not require time. What does take place is, once again, a conversion of energy, or a change of vibratory rates, or action appearing in change of form. The illustration, of course, cannot be pushed too far, but it is difficult to do without some degree of picture-thinking, and it often helps to simplify matters. This same picture of concentric spheres is useful in understanding the "Fortean falls", of all kinds of stuff 'from the skies' -- a well-attested phenomenon. It fits in, too, with the remarkable graph or sketch of the earth and the proximate etheric zones, given by Etheric communicators to Dr. Gerald Light, and reproduced at the end of this booklet.

There is a very profound occult saying, that "you are where your consciousness is" (for if not, where are you?). It is just as true to say, that a disc or ethership IS wherever its vibration rate puts it, on Venus or Mars or on our earth or within it, or five miles deep undersea. Etheric matter can be 'tuned in', and here and there are matters of frequencies, densities, wave lengths - not of spacial position in a three-dimensional void!! Of course there is no end to the metaphysical subtleties involved in all this, or to speculative scientific thinking either - or to our ignorance. But the human race en masse now seems to be getting its ABC instruction - and perhaps a few of us may get as far as D and E - which, at any rate, should bespeak an intelligent hearing for our "4-D" explanations.

Science is only now beginning its exploration of sub-atomic matter; along with this must go new concepts of space, time, the ether(s), tele - or apportation, the energic character of thinking - and also of high importance, the reality of communication with etheric peoples, the Star-Wanderers and Guardians, and with wise and good people of our own race, who are in the regions of the so-called dead but indeed very much alive - far more alive than we are here, cloistered in self-conceit and ignorance.

It may also facilitate a sympathetic understanding of the "Communications" if we supply a brief biographical data concerning the Controls. As to the meetings themselves, they are always held in full light, without any formalities or special restrictions; the intermediary (medium) sits behind a small table and simply 'goes to sleep', and one Control after another talks through him, with free exchange of questions and answers. The personalities are very distinct and fully integrated, and have been extensively questioned by scientists, linguists and research workers. There are no physical phenomena in the usual meaning of that expression. Meetings have been held at least once a week for some eight years past, and in all the large cities of the Pacific Slope.

BIOGRAPHICAL NOTES CONCERNING
THE MARK PROBERT CONTROLS

LINGFORD, CHARLES: One of the earliest Controls. 'Passed over' at turn of the present century and while still a young man. At one time a dancer and entertainer. Unmarried. He has a clever and active intelligence and a fine sense of humor. Occupies himself with music and painting and also with scientific and philosophic matters - as his quoted remarks indicate.

EDISON, THOMAS. Too well known to call for comment here. He has communicated through many different mediums and keeps up his scientific interest and work.

LAO-TSE or LAO-TZU: b. 604 B.C. (encyc.), but "lived between 550-600 B.C. in a town called K'uhsien. He belonged to a wealthy and educated family, and had no need to work for the Imperial Library, yet spent much time there poring over the books. He later became a roaming sage. Actually did no writing at all, but his sayings were compiled by his disciples. Had a wife and seven children, and according to custom several concubines. At about fifty years of age he abandoned his family and followers and was taken into the mystical school of the White Brotherhood. He died smiling happily at the age of eighty-two."* (an extraordinary intellect and a truly great philosopher; a central figure in Taoism. ml)

LO SUN YAT: "In the year 1650 A.D. a boy child was born to a very poor family by the name of Chui Fu Yang. He was of such delicate build it was thought he should have been a girl, until it was discovered his body contained both sexes. This was thought to be an ill omen and his father intended to drown him, but his mother secreted him. One day while wandering about the countryside with him, she encountered a kindly priest who offered to take good care of him. At the age of ten years he was taken to Tibet, where he stayed until he was twenty, becoming a lama of the Yellow Robe. Unable to tolerate the corruption of the lamasaries, he fled to India, where he was taken into the mystery School of the Light, and where he died sixty years later, a venerated and much-loved Master of the Order.

PROFESSOR (DR.) ALFRED LUNTZ:

"This personality was born in 1812 and died in 1893. He was of English and German parentage and was born in North London. After completing his secondary education at Eton he enrolled at the University of Heidelberg, where he studied philosophy and comparative religion, and

*NOTE: Sentences in quotation marks were recently dictated to Mark Probert for purposes of this book. All of the data, however, has come from the Controls at one time or another. ml

Oxford, where he received his Ph.D. degree. He was ordained a priest at the age of about 40 into the Anglican communion. He was not surprised to find that he had survived death, but was stunned by the realization that there was no heaven or hell as he had so eloquently taught and believed. He became a member of the Inner Circle of the Mark Probert controls in the year 1946."

RAMOND NATALLI:

"This personality was born in 1598 and died in 1652. He was an astronomer and belonged to the Royal House of Astronomy at Rome, Italy" (Astronomer Royal? m.). "He was a student of law, a close friend of the famous Galileo, and secretly fought the bloody hand of the Inquisition. He was himself an agnostic. He was pleasantly surprised to discover he had survived physical death, and continued to pursue his astronomical studies on the astral. After being in the astral for about two years he discovered two things of great interest: (1) that sun spots were atomic storms and that (2) atoms consist of photons of varied frequency levels moving in a series of quantum arcs."

ARAKASHI: Very little seems to be known about this personality. All that the Inner Circle can or will say, is that he was a Guru (holy man), who lived and died in the Punjab district of India c. 1320-98 A.D. - teachings were Buddhistic.

RAMA KALOHA: Very little information has been given about this personality, apart from the fact that he was a Guru and a Hindu of great age, who appeared from time to time in the Indian Parliament when critical issues were at stake. His first noticeable appearance was in the latter half of the 17th c., and the last when Mahatma Ghandi was killed and Nehru came into power.

THE YADA DI SHI'ITE: The title of Yada means High Priest, and also "spirit life"; Shi'ite means clan, also "mystic Order". "This personality was born in the city of Kaoti (City of Temples) in a civilization called YU (or Yuga, Vast Body), consisting of some 180 million people, and existing in the Himalayan Mountains a half-million years ago. The Yada was taken from his mother as a baby and reared in the temple to become a Kata (Priest) and later a Yada. He was killed in a violent quake that destroyed the YU civilization and 80 millions of its people. Yada was then about 34 years old and the YU civilization was 1024 years old."

THE MAHARAJAH NATCHA TRAMALAKI: "The story concerning this personality is that he was born of an English mother and an Indian father, in the year 1848, in Dacca, India. His parents were wealthy and owned a large estate, and the son was sent to study medicine at Oxford University. But he was a poet and philosopher, and after taking his final degree in medicine (to please his father) he suddenly disappeared. He is said to have spent some ten years in travels in remote regions of the world, and died in his home in Bombay about 1915."

'All questions pose more questions' (says the Rajah) - 'and all
answers are personal opinions - and the only sound rule and reply to
life's problems is to <u>question nothing</u>, but to face all situations with
detachment...'

- - - - - - - - - - -

It has been repeatedly pointed out by the Controls, that complete
and perfect identification of any communicator is impossible, in the
nature of the case. It involves the concept of what constitutes identity, and even on our own plane the best that can be done is to estab-
lish a 'reasonable conviction'. The Controls assert that it is within
the power of every individual's Higher Self to reproduce "every trait,
memory, and characteristic" of any deceased person, and though the
probabilities may be overwhelming, they must still, in theory at least,
fall short of final and unquestionable 'proof'.

ml

The   Inner   Circle
Communications

Deep Trance   Mediumship
of
Mark Probert

Charles Lingford, Control (1947)

When will you people learn that there are worlds within
worlds - that the etheric worlds interpenetrate with your plane
and with each other? I know I should not be sticking my neck
out by talking so much about these saucers, as you call them,
at least until I have investigated more fully. But they are
not craft constructed on your planet*, nor is it necessary to
assume that they come from any other planet. It seems impossible to get it through your heads, that objects can pass from
an etheric to another level of matter and will then appear to
materialize there. Then they disappear by dematerialization,
returning to an etheric condition.

This is a perfect analogue to the materializations wit-
nessed in the seance room, which many of your learned men bear
witness to. Not only do human forms materialize, but solid
objects appear 'miraculously', and often these are brought from
long distances. You call them apports, but an apport is de-
materialized so that only the etheric pattern remains, and then
the original atoms are reassembled in the pattern or mould and
you have a materialized object. Well, these 'saucers' that
puzzle you so much come out of an etheric world also, and can
return to it. The purpose of these visitors is simply to com-
pel your attention, to wake you up."'"

(* Now widely believed — January 1957. At present
writing the 'purpose' seems to be 'regulatory action' of
some type, concerning our planetary affairs, and probably
connected with seismic conditions also. ml)

There will be many strange sky appearances, as we have
often told you before in these meetings. Watch for them. These
'saucers' make their great speed partly because of their peculiar bun shape and peculiar motion...The wilful ignorance and
hostility of your time toward etheric and astral studies is appalling. These visitors are not excarnate humans, but live in
their own world, made of stuff which your senses cannot directly perceive, and which you therefore childishly imagine cannot
be there at all.

Charles Lingford, Control. Nov., 1953

Whatever is subsequently discovered in regard to this
particular kind of sky phenomena, one outstanding fact will be
that space is not the vacuous thing it has long been considered.

Also another kind of phenomenon, quite unthinkable in the eyes of most of your physical scientists, called teleportation, will have to be studied more widely and seriously. The facts are that no matter how distant one body may be from another in the stellar spaces, "Nature" has a method of moving all manner of things from one of these bodies to another - called teleportation -- all of which disproves the statement that 'what goes up must come down.'

It appears rather strange to me that so few people have thought of connecting the 'discs' with the endless other sky phenomena, such as are found in great number in the books of 'tongue-in-cheek' Charles Fort. When it is mentioned that these things fall, fly, walk, or crawl out of other space - times you have referred to as the ethers, everyone cries -- "but they are solid!" Well, hallelujah, and bless you, my child! So they are! And so also is your earth and the billions of other bodies that go to make up the many island universes. But again, all depends on what one means by the word 'solid'. The term simply refers to one of many states of what is loosely called matter at some given time. Neither your earth or any other body in space came out of a 'void' or state of nothingness. And to say that any of it was spawned from a field of 'primordial astral dust' (science), or that the Lord made it in six days and finished it on the seventh (religion) is enough to set one into hysterical laughter. That 'primordial dust', notwithstanding that one may call it pure energy, still has to come from something, and that something needs to be particulate in nature, and is so.

The fact that the study of what are called light and quanta seemed to take away from the particulate theory and add something called wave does not change the fact that ALL is of particulate nature, or the law of change would be invalid. I think, however, the greatest trouble in the field of physics is the present meaning attached to the word atom. An atom is not something in itself that can be broken up into parts. To pour a stream of neutron bullets at an atom of uranium does not smash it or knock a piece of it off, for actually, while I do state in a very definite manner that all is particulate, we must not think of that word as implying a final bit of something, but rather as a field of motion and frequency degree extended or contracted in a given radius -- as, for instance, we may say when an atom bomb is exploded: "A dwarf star in the solar system of the uranium universe has become a giant nova" - which simply means that a field of energy has become more extended in its mode of motion, and needs a larger volume of space to operate in. Nevertheless, whatever measurable extent a body may be operating in, it is discharging from itself other bands of energy in an ever-widening radius as infinitum, and up to the present your scientific minds have not devised an instrument sufficiently sensitive to detect these fields of action.

It is out of these that not only the Discs make their appearance into your lower vibrations, but also such things as ice falls, rains of blood, and materializations of objects and materializations of former living things.

Lingford, con., July, 1947

(Questions and Answers)

Lingford: Yes, I heard FGH's opinion. In the course of time you will find that these things (Discs) will tell their own story. You know from your reading and study that there have been many such phenomena. Just now you are having them in large numbers and over a wide region, because the world is in a sense ready for them. All we need now is to be pushed a little bit and we will wake up.

(Question: You have no reason at this time, then, to change your interpretation of them?)

No, I have not. Do you suppose for a moment that any actual material thing such as you know could rip and tear across the sky without burning up? I don't mean to say it is not material, but the material is such it can stand the heat and speed.

(Question: Does this construction material exist on our plane? An alloy, perhaps?)

Yes, a kind of alloy. There will be more of them, and perhaps of various kinds.

(Q. Are you familiar with the doctrine of the Lokas?)

No. The only thing I can say about these things (Discs) is that the condition or state from which they come is etheric. It is a materialization and dematerialization.

(Q. Is there any relation between the discs and the things that have been found (fallen)?)

There are various ways of running things by remote control
other than those you know of. There are energies yet unknown
to science. Do you remember the pictures Dr. Cosman had? Do
you recall seeing those things in the sky? They are the same
kind of beings as created these phenomena (of the discs). Did
you note in the pictures how giant of size they are? These are
etheric dwellers who have not known physical life. I am referring to your 'flying saucers'. They come out of that plane of
existence.

(Q. Do some of the discs carry a crew?)

The large ones, yes; the small ones, no. (Q). Yes, these
are controlled from the craft that carries the crew. Some
break away and then become limp like paper and vanish. (Q).
No, they do not return to another vibration rate in such case.
The energy goes back whence it came; they disintegrate, lose
identity. This explains what happens to those that appear to
land. The force and the structure disintegrate.

(Q). If there are beings in a disc which disintegrates,
they simply go back to the etheric world from which they
emerged. (Q). No, you will get no information from your
"higher-ups". No, they are not being withdrawn, they are being
explained away!! However, they will carry on until explanations
run out and people become curious again.

(Q. No reports for several days ...?)

They have shifted their field of operation. They have the
world to cover. There is a reason for everything and I believe
one reason for the discs is to show the people of the world
there are ways of travelling faster and eliminating friction.
They may allow one or two of these things to land so that they
can be examined and experimented on. In that way you will find
how to build craft that will travel out into space and maybe
you can find a new planet to start new wars upon.

Yes, I believe man will abandon this planet, but not for
many years to come. Nature is vast and man fits in as a part
of it. He may try to destroy himself but he will be unsuccess-
ful and it will make him unhappy. But a time will come, and
science knows it, when if the human race hopes to survive it
will have to have a new planet to survive on.

(Q. Do you recognize the existence of etheric planets?)

Oh yes, there are etheric planets, and then gaseous planets that are just forming into solid material. New ones are being made all the time. Yes, they might be said to originate in the Lokas ... You know, I'm getting tired. The trouble in my world is the same as in yours - a great deal of talk and nothing really satisfactory. You will find that condition in all worlds and all states of consciousness.

(Q. No heaven, then, Lingford?)

If there is, you would not be happy there. Without boredom there would be a state of inertia. Man must be unhappy in order to exist. The moment he becomes perfectly happy he becomes non-existent ...

Some time ago one of your Controls hinted that man was an awesome creature in many ways. I could never begin to tell you how awesome he really is. Horror upon horror is in him - and beauty beyond conception also - his many-sidedness is appalling ... I want to add about the discs, we haven't given any wrong information. The predictions of that woman, about the discs being of Russian origin, are incorrect. There is no new information at present, but the Russian source is ridiculous. I do know that they come from the etheric world.

- - - - - -

(The reader will again note the date of this last foregoing section. The Lingford Control had evidently not grasped the magnitude of the Disc incursion or its deeper significance - at least as these are now partially understood. But nothing in his earlier statement has been discredited by later events, and his later 1953 statement bears it out.

(I here repeat a point made elsewhere - that the possibility of obtaining dependable information by paranormal means such as deep-trance mediumship, is nearly as important as the incursion of the Guardians itself. The whole of this booklet is an unanswerable argument in behalf of this tremendous certainty. It is not a new thing in the world, of course, yet improbable and fantastic to our pseudo-science and sapient Western culture). ml

<u>THOMAS EDISON, Control</u>

1947

Well, how am I doing now? (referring to difficulty in control). No, I have never spoken through a medium this way before, but I did speak once through a trumpet at Lily Dale (a spiritualist center in New York state). I was Thomas Edison during my life on your plane. I made many secret experiments in the effort to recapture and reproduce sounds made in past time, and preserved in the ether. I still believe that this is possible and that it will be done. At the time I only had a hypothesis to work on, but one often has to use a hypothesis in order to have a starting point.

(Q. -- as to how he happened to come to the medium) -- Well, you have a very unusual group over here, who are interested in the particular type of seance which you carry on. Continue with this work and you will probably get some very strange news. If you publicize it you will be ridiculed, but I was ridiculed too.

About these discs that are stirring up so much comment - I'm a little afraid they are going to make trouble. (Q.) I mean they may start a panic. My ideas about them are much the same as those given by Lingford. They are etheric in nature, and they materialize spontaneously upon entering the vibration rate of your world of dense matter. I think this is going to stir up a hell of a lot of trouble. The great trouble, of course, is with your scientists -- they can't get into the right way of thinking about such problems.

(Q.) They happen to be appearing just now, because your world is now in that phase of thought. Do you understand what I am getting at? There will be many other types of strange sky craft also. That Corrida (Kareeta) you wrote about last year was the same type, etheric construction. It was an experimental craft. (Q.) These people are much like yourselves, but they are much bigger.

(Q.) Yes, I think it might be right to say they come from the Lokas. No, they are not astral, and not from any of the planets you know about. They come from an etheric planet which your senses do not perceive. Some of the discs carry a crew, but others are managed by remote control . . . . ..

LAO-TSO, CONTROL

1948

"They have often come simply in quest of knowlecge, just as you make expeditions to far-off places, to the Polar regions or to Central Asia --

"They are not here with intent to interfere in your affairs - nevertheless, if there is another world war, employing nuclear energies, they may be forced to intervene. The release of atomic forces has disturbed their sphere of existence rather seriously.

"Let it be understood that if ever such intervention becomes necessary, it will be wholly impersonal. There will be no taking of sides. It is contrary to the Law, that any one plane should interfere with the processes by which another works out its destiny.

"They are vastly your superiors in science - though every plane has its special forms of development and progress, so that we speak of differences, but not often of superiority or inferiority.

"The Ethereans are large people, up to fifteen feet in height. I would say that they belong to the human order of evolution - that is, you would not call them Devas or Nature Spirits. Yet the great forms you have seen and photographed, in the clouds and on the surface of the earth also, somewhat resemble them.

"You ask why they are now suddenly present in large numbers. I shall tell you. Always, when a civilization, a culture has reached its height and is destined to collapse, the Ethereans have appeared in numbers. They come to make an examination and final record, for their own knowledge, of the status of that civilization - somewhat as you might do with disappearing tribes and races. And it is true also that they have been alerted and disturbed by your release of atomic energies. But all past civilizations and races have had their day, and failed in some way, and passed out of earth existence. So with your civilization. The Etherean people came, and observed, and made their historical records. So they come now.

LO SUN YAT, Control

August, 1948

(Q.) You were speaking of the etheric regions -- will you talk more of that? You know probably that we are having strange sky appearances which, we have been told, originate on etheric levels. We are told there are whole races, civilizations, etc., on these levels, but there seems very little definite information on these regions.)

To me, the etheric regions are the region of <u>life</u>; the astral regions of what you call death is the waiting-hall. If man desires, he can leave the astral after a period of time and enter into the etheric life, and he need not come back here to your physical world if he does not wish, but he can go on to the higher realms of this etheric world. This which I term the 'etheric' is the home out of which all physical manifestations come; so it is not to be wondered at that now and then, when necessary, there are projections of various forms into your physical state of consciousness.

(Q. Would you say that the elementals, the devas, etc., live in the etheric region?)

Yes, but of a different kind. It is also not right to call it 'low' -- it is merely a different plane of existence, which Nature devised for them.

(Q. These regions interpenetrate with ours? Answer: Yes.

(Q. What is the nature of the Etherians? Answer: Just like your physical world -- not a replica, but along similar lines.

(Q. But they have not been on our plane?)

Not those on the higher etheric. I do not know but that at some time some of them may wish to enter into your plane of physical existence; but I do not think they come through your way of birth, but through projection.

(Q. Will you tell us more about the astral and etheric; and also why anyone should want to come back to the earth? Also, we do not understand the use of the word 'death' for astral.

It is, in my opinion, a bad term; it is demoralizing to the average person -- but it is not anything like what the word implies. 'Death' -- no; it is merely a different form of living. But this door between the astral and etheric and the physical is always left open, because man so desires it. He must have channels between his worlds if he is to learn and progress in knowledge.

It is only because the physical or chemical body seems to go through such distressing states that one often says, 'I have no desire to come back into the physical.' Now, I feel that if conditions were so that the chemical substances of the body were not subject to these distressing conditions one would enjoy physical living as much as on the other planes. It is only the desire to escape pain, want, and poverty.

(Q. No doubt; but our conditions probably never will be as good as that.

No -- not for those at large; but after you have learned to have complete control and govern the body, then you become a joyful person on any plane of existence, because all planes do have their drawbacks and difficulties. Therefore it pays great dividends to become familiar with the physical body.

(Q. Would you say that the etheric planes we have been speaking of correspond with the 'lokas' of Oriental philosophy? Answer: Yes.

(Q. Are there seven or eight lokas as they say? Yes, there are. You see, man enters these various states of consciousness according to his desires.

(Q. But we have understood that man does not enter into the etheric at all, but into the astral? Answer: He does on his return, though.

(Q. He has an etheric body, then? Yes. It is in that state of consciousness that he starts building the thought stresses for his physical manifestation.

(Q. We are also taught that on leaving this plane, the entity enters an etheric body for a short time and then it is discarded. Is that correct?

This etheric body is discarded, but not as you think. It instantly disintegrates. There is no shell left, no period of time when it floats about aimlessly.

(Q. But there is this time when it is in an etheric body?
Yes, but it is in this state that he often goes to sleep.

(Q. The materializations of the seance room apparently
depend upon ectoplasm -- is there such a thing as ectoplasm
that can be drawn from all organic matter? Answer: Yes.

(Q. And from inorganic matter also? Answer: Yes, all
matter contains this.

(Q. All matter has what you would call a dynamic etheric
force? Answer: Yes.

(Q. Is this what you would call an etheric double? Answer: I will ask you to excuse me now. I shall answer your
question at some other time.

(Included here because the references to the Etheric world and
bodies are obviously relevant. - M.L.)

Professor Alfred Luntz - 1948

"Let us turn back our minds in what you perceive as time,
even to the world's beginnings. If you were looking with the
physical eye, you would see nothing but what would appear to
you as a vast endless void; but let us use an eye that is of a
higher rate of vibration and look again. Now what would you
see? A sight so astounding, so majestic that were you to see
it while in the physical body and unprepared, you would indeed
go stark mad. For now you are looking into the Etheric world.
The size alone of all in it would stagger your imagination.
The vibrating, pulsating, iridescent colors, teeming with plant
life, the animals and birds; the size and beauty of buildings,
libraries, lecture halls, schools of learning, vast cathedrals,
giant organs, orchestras consisting of every known instrument
on your earth plane and many, many more you, as yet, know nothing of -- tens of thousands playing at one time and the music
coming from them would make you want to weep your life away
with its power and sweetness of tone and perfect harmony; men
and women of great height and stature, perfect of body and mind,
going about in flowing robes of brilliant colors - - - some
with mighty heads of golden hair, red hair and black hair flowing down their backs in living, gleaming waves, and rich flowing beards that look like fine-spun silk; stately women with
skin like living satin and glowing with health.

"The air you would breathe would be purer than a babe's
breath, for the air in this world is not particulate, as your
scientists feel they know that word. Things do not move around
in the manner that one may call directional motion, but by
vibration motion only. Perhaps I may make such a condition a
bit more clear by saying, 'Being that in essence all forces are
really one force, when a thing or person wishes to move, the
wish automatically merges the energy force of that thing or
person into the thing it or he desires to move to; in other
words, it is the motion of the neutron and the proton -- a
complete exchange of energies, one thing becoming the other
thing.

"It is only when coming down into the lower etheric that
one begins to run into the first stages of particulate substances or directional motion. In the physical, in order for one
substance to become something else, there is a change or a re-
arrangement of the atomic pattern. This is the beginning of

what I call <u>directional</u> motion. It is at a period slightly
before directional motion that physical man has, for the most
part, lost his ability to control substance with mental energy
and must of necessity revert to his hands -- the hands being
extensions of the mind.

"Note that I say 'for the most part' and not completely;
for it is a known fact that there are in India, even in your
time, men who have so mastered themselves that they can cause
flowers and other plants to grow and blossom right before your
eyes. Notice the method employed by these men to accomplish
this: a complete trance state. And why a trance state? Simply
that <u>they</u> may become the <u>plant</u>. By that I mean their mind substance may enter into the mind substance of the plant seed.

"Perhaps it would be clearer to you if I explained it
thusly: When you, my friend, go into a trance so that we may
use your physical body, you are in reality becoming the one who
appears to talk through you."

-- ("Magic Bag" -- Part I, pages 4-5).

Prof. Luntz, Control

- 1948 -

Yes, a night or two ago I wrote through the boy a little
about etheric life, but it is too lengthy a subject to go into
at present. I can touch upon it, and that is all.

(Q. I made the point here a little while ago that we ex-
pect many inquiries as to the people of the etheric realms. We
shall be grateful if you can tell us anything about them --
their culture, if any, etc.

No doubt you have seen pictures and read many stories of
the 'little people', the fairies, the nature spirits. They
are of the Lower Etheric. In the Higher Etheric you will find
people much like yourself, but of mightier proportions. Their
bodies are much like yours in the physical plane.

(Q. A name is given to them? Answer: Not so far as I
now know. I shall have to do a little research on that.

(Q. It seems strange that in all the libraries of occult
thought there is so little about them. Have they ever been

investigated from our side?

Yes, by a few who know something of the deeper side of occult life. The references in writing are very few, but I think you will find some of them in India.

Q. This is an important matter, it seems to us.

Yes, it is. In my research in the matter, I find it a most glorious world, and that all life -- your vast systems of stars and suns and what not -- spring from it. There is a great deal for me to write about, but I am sometimes almost a-fraid to put this matter out, because to the mind of the earth people it is so fantastic. It is, I am sure, almost incompre-hensible.

Q. Now that we are dealing with 'flying discs' and such etheric phenomena we will need much knowledge to answer ques-tions.

I want to say one thing: this thing that your scientists have looked for and called ether does not exist either in your plane or mine, but in this etheric plane.

(Q. But ether permeates our dense world? All ethers are particulate, not homogeneous?

That is one of your difficulties -- because on this partic-ular plane of consciousness -- I mean, the etheric world -- it is not particulate as you understand that word.

(Q. You mean it is what we call homogeneous? Answer: Yes.

(Q. I have asked if there is a continuum and received a flat no. Answer: Because they do not know.

(Q. Is motion possible in a homogeneous medium? Answer: Yes. What I am trying to say is that it is particulate as you view it.

(Q. You speak of this etheric world -- is it just another plane of consciousness above yours? Answer: It is not what you would call above; it is merely a different level of cons-ciousness.....

(Q. There is motion and there are living entities in a

continuum of energy substance?

Yes. When I wrote through the boy (Mark Probert) about the vast symphony orchestra of ten thousand pieces -- does that not stun your mind? What I am getting at is that there must be motion in order to play such instruments.

(Q. I asked that because we do not see how a continuum can move; we think only of parts moving.

Exactly so. In all states of consciousness there is motion. Without motion there is nothing. Speaking, too, of light -- light is a constant. It does not in our field, the astral or the etheric, travel at any speed, but is a constant, a constant now -- an inward vibration.

(Q. Our mathematics cannot take into account a continuum that moves.

It is an inward vibration, not an outward motion. These two, material science and metaphysics, are really one, but they seem to work against each other. Laboratory motion is more what you would call -- let me see -- motion by dots, instead of by lines; you understand?

(Q. Yes, but the subject is perhaps too vast ---

(Q. Can you tell us a little more about the dots and lines? Answer: In line-motion you have light being, or seeming to be, projected from one point to another. In dot vibration, you have single bodies glowing within themselves periodically; or perhaps that would come under the quantum theory.

(Q. The quantum theory is used in television, because of the use of the living and glowing dots -- that is what you are trying to get across? Answer: It is a very difficult thing to explain.

(Q. But it will be easier as television becomes understandable. Answer: Yes, it will.

Prof. Luntz, Control (cont'd)

I will change the subject for a moment, and because Rama Ka Lo cannot come tonight, I will speak a few words about the 'flying discs'. I hope it will be interesting to you, because

it is important. You have been told by your authorities that
you have 'spots before the eyes', and I think just now must be
a good time for the optician's business. 'Reason, pure reason!' your scientists demand. If they had left off that 'pure'
it would have been fine! Discs, space ships -- or perhaps
illusions, mass hysterics, mass hysteria! Until they appeared,
no one had hysteria. Now, I am not criticizing your Government;
but in this country the people are supposed to be the government. Are you being protected because you are not quite strong
enough to face the true knowledge?

It would be easy enough to say these things all come from
the planets. Of course that would give your astronomers a
slight headache, seeing they have put these at such great distances -- thousands and thousands of what you call 'light
years'. Is there not something closer than planets? Imagination?
(I said that first, because I knew you would soon say 'imagination'). If you are not worried about these things, that is
quite all right -- because you certainly have enough to worry
about already. But these great craft come out of what we of
the 'Inner Circle' call the Etheric.

Prof. Alfred Luntz. Communication of Jan., 1953

It appears that the Disc incidents are coming to a head
of some kind, and it may seem to you that some of our statements are on the threshold of being discredited. We would not
mind any seeming loss of face for ourselves but we would depre-
cate it for you. Hence we reiterate once more, that while Dr.
Williamson or Mr. Adamski may have talked with a being from
some other planet, and that Dr. Williamson is in radio contact
with such beings, nevertheless the majority of the Disc phenomena are of etheric nature, or not of your time dimension.

These beings may prove to be quite solid and capable of
walking about on the earth, and they may claim to exist on Venus or any other planet, in or out of your solar system - but
this does not imply that they are in their structural units
humans of the same order as you earth people, or that they lack
the ability to convert their seeming solids to invisible stuff
at will. Nor does it disprove that they are Guardians not only
of the earth but of the whole solar system in which your
planet exists.

In speaking of etheric culture, you know of course that we

must do so in a metaphysical way. There is considerable knowledge of the etheric worlds among secret occult Orders, but the
lay mind knows nothing of this and can never know of it.

Etherian culture may mean little more than a fantasy to
you, but if you pursue the subject you will come to understand
that your world of matter is really a rarefaction of the ether,
spawned into being by the forces of Involution, not of Evolution, and that it came out of the Etheric. Man himself is an
etheric being and a space being. Long before your earth came
into form man was moving from one planet and one solar system
to another.

Symbols have many meanings. Those on the sandals have
all the meanings found by you, and yet many more.

These people are Guardians and move from one planet to
another. If one said that he 'came from Venus' he was giving a
kind of general direction - as you might say, 'I came from the
Middle West'. Their forms are different while in passage on
account of gravitational pulls and other conditions.

Prof. Luntz, Control (cont'd)

- 1950 -

Now, if you can sit here and listen to my voice speaking
to you through this instrument whom we call 'The Boy' (because we are all so many, many years older than he), and think
it is quite all right, nothing too much out of the ordinary,
then how can you consider that great civilization called the
Etheric as fantastic, impossible? What is impossible?

(Answer from listeners, "Nothing!")

That is the understanding we want to arrive at: that
whatever man wishes, he can do.

These craft come for what purpose? Primarily to make
notes on the physical condition of the Earth itself, as well
as the state of advancement of your scientific approach to
life. Whenever a civilization reaches a great state of advancement in every line, that civilization has reached its
peak -- and I do not know why the present civilization should
think it is any different from any other civilization and

escape decay -- or, to put it better -- <u>change</u>.

When these Etherians gather as much information as needed, they hold it until such time as that civilization falls. And when another starts to rise again and after it has attained a certain degree of advancement, these things are handed down to the Earth people again through the channels of mystic organizations.

There is much to learn, friends -- much! A great philosopher once said, (and I don't mean to be trite about it) - 'It is later than you think!' Does that sound ominous? I don't mean it that way; it is only that each one of you has not much time for awakening to the greatness of yourselves.

To give you but a short resume: These craft are operated by the little-known laws of molecular action called <u>heat</u> and <u>cold</u>. You are watching one right now. Why do we move this boy's body back and forth this way? Because all bodies that move create heat. Every slightest motion creates heat to a degree. We use that energy, and we can, when we are through, return it, to a large extent, so the boy suffers no particular ill. His wife's energy we use also, for always there is a positive and a negative force to life. Have any of you questions to ask?

(Q. Our present physics combines the wave-motion with the old molecular motion.

We say that light does not travel, but that certain particles change their rates of motion at certain times, and these changes create a vibratory rate that causes what I can only call a <u>reflection</u>. I do not know that I make myself clear?

(Q. Is light a continuous state in the ethers? Answer: Yes, it is.

(Q. What is darkness, then? Answer: A different state of molecular motion. Yes, co-existing with light.

(Q. And the day-and-night idea is merely psychological?

It is. Let us suppose there is a molecule here -- at one moment its vibration is low; it creates no light. Then, through throwing off a kind of radiation, it produces what is called heat. There are two kinds of heat -- white and black.

(Q. Does it do that of itself, or is it controlled by something else?

Sir, if I had a physical brain, it would burst under that question. I am afraid I would have to give some considered thought to that, and confer with the 'Inner Circle'. I am not quite sure of it myself.

- - - - - - - - - -

(With reference to the confused use of suns, planets, stars, and other verbal inaccuracies, we should keep in mind that much of this is rather rapid conversational exchange, and that Professor Luntz is not trying to speak with scientific precision, for the moment at least). ml

Ramon Natalli, Control

- 1949 -

Here is something else we wish you to think upon: For
many years now, most of your scientists who go into the investigation of physical phenomena have not seemed to realize
that the "matter" which goes to make up the shape and forms on
the unseen level is much <u>denser</u> than the matter on the physical plane. It is assumed that, because your solids can be
turned into liquids, and then into gases, and that certain of
these gases become invisible to the physical eye -- due to
wider separation of their component parts and the greater os-
cillation of their atomic motion -- that a similar condition
exists on other planes of consciousness. If this were so, how
could a disembodied entity take <u>your</u> physical matter and spread
it over his body? No, this could not be done if your matter
were heavier and denser than ours. One could not spread heavier and denser matter on other matter that was less dense than
itself. It could not hold up under the strain.....

The fact is, however, that the electronic bodies that
whirl around the atom or nucleus of our matter are gathered
closer to the nucleus, due to the lowering of heat radiation
from the nucleus. This constriction of the electronic field
of our atom gives our bodies a greater density and elasticity
in comparison to yours. It also explains why our atom of matter can pass right on through the electronic field of the atom
of your matter without disturbing its field.

The teleportation of matter and the act of bringing one
form of matter through another seems to cause a great amount of
amazement among you. The facts are, however, that both of these
forms of activity are normal functions in nature. When you
discover, as you will in time, how closely interrelated are
mind and matter, or the various planes of the unseen and your
physical-chemical world, you will then understand the many
methods of teleportation.

One of these methods is the reduction of a physical body,
animate or inanimate, to its etheric state by the condensing
of its atomic structure. In this form it can be transported to
any point in or throughout the vast universe. As a rule, teleportation is the work of etheric beings, though sometimes of
an advanced discarnate spirit, and at other times it is

accomplished by foolish spirit beings who have learned how to
manipulate physical matter and who, not knowing the great good
they could do with that knowledge, squander their energy by
using it to frighten or amuse those still in the body. Your
"spirit" in the "Bell Witch Case", however, was not a discarnate entity but an etheric being who had been cast down into
the Low Etheric from the High Etheric plane. He had a great
deal of good as well as evil in him. He had committed some un-
pardonable deeds, and was therefore cast out of his high state
for a given period of time. So he spoke truth when he said
that he had roamed Heaven and Hell for millions of years. His
"Hell" was the coming down into the Low Etheric.

Man, in any state, is a child of impulse. We all act in
and by impulse, but sometimes we let go and allow these little
motions in thought to drive us to what eventually proves our
undoing.

Now, let us turn back to the topic of matter and some of
its different forms of activity. In reducing formed matter to
a formless state, you are merely sending it back a few stages
to its original condition, but there is no physical scientist
who knows how to take it back to its original condition; for if
he could accomplish this, the bit of substance that he so reduced would escape him entirely, and the only machine that could
bring it back to the place where he could come into physical
contact with it again would be through the mind of certain individuals, working in conjunction with the brain.

In reducing a solid to a gas you are not causing that substance to be anything other than it was before; you are merely
breaking up and scattering its component parts, thereby giving
it different shape or form. Ice and invisible steam are not
two different things, but the same thing in a different rate of
motion of its parts.

The more a physical-chemical substance is divided, the
more dense its remaining parts become, and therefore the greater must be the force or work done on it to split it again. The
reason for this condition seems to be that the gravitational
pressure of the ether, in which all matter floats, becomes
greater as the parts are divided. The raising of this pressure
is always equal to the parts taken away. This is why it has
taken such tremendous force to split your atom.

It must also be known that the more matter is divided and

subdivided, the greater the radiation heat it creates within itself. Never can matter be reduced to the point of one. All nature works with two or more energies and forces working in harmony -- and when I use the word "two" I do so figuratively; for truly the act of division, in its deeper sense, is maya, or illusion, for we can never really either divide or add to anything. All we can do is to bring about a changed condition of activity. And if we bring about this change before its natural time, we will have to hold on constantly to the method we used to make that change, or that which was so changed will automatically revert to its original state.

* * * * * * * * *

One of the deepest mysteries that confronts scientific minds is the origin of matter. I am afraid this is not a problem that can be answered by your physical science, but rather by metaphysical science; and I am sure the latter would say matter has no point of origin, as man understands that word origin. Matter just is. Let us suppose, however, that there was such a thing as a point in space out of which matter was spawned: the point itself would have to be of some kind of matter which man could recognize and comprehend. And, again, whether this point were submicroscopic in size or a hundred billion miles extending in all directions, one could not say that its location in space was here or there unless there was another body standing somewhere in relation to it. When we consider this, we can then understand to a better degree why a dot or a point cannot, of itself, have an existence.

However, this is true also of a line or a plane, for a line consists of a series of dots, and a plane a series of lines that are made up of dots. If, then, a dot or a point is non-existent in itself, the same must be true of a line or a plane. Therefore, matter can only be a production of the mind.

Ramon Natalli, Control

- 1950 -

(Q. Would you care to speak of what looked to us like a great explosion on Mars a day or so ago?

It was -- a great and terrible explosion. It came from a gigantic volcano that has not been active for hundreds and hundreds of years. There was an eruption over some 9,000 miles of land, and a terrible, terrible 'quake.

(Q. Were there inhabitants who were injured or killed by it?

Not inhabitants like yourselves, but life forms of a lower nature. There has been some talk about sky-phenomena, about things that fly in your skies; some seem to think that these come from Mars or Venus -- they do, but not from the terrestrial Mars or Venus. There is around every planet -- and, for that matter, around every body in the vast heavens -- an etheric world. These bodies govern, or are governed by those in the etheric world. They are under their direct and watchful eye.

(Q. Are you saying that what we call the planet Mars and Venus are under the control of their etheric counterparts? -- Answer: Yes, they are.

(Q. And is that true of our planet? Answer: Yes -- these intelligences, I believe, some of you call the Group Soul. It is not too good an expression; it does not explain things.

(Q. Would you say that all of these skycraft come from the etheric region of some particular planet? Answer: I most assuredly would.

(Q. And will you tell us which planet? Answer: I think, Venus -- In fact, those who constructed these so-called 'Disc ships' copied the design of their craft after the body Venus with its outer vibrating disc or ring.

(Q. Are we to infer that the disc-type of craft came, then, from the etheric region of Venus? Answer: Yes.

(Q. And the others come from other planets? Mars, for example? Answer: Yes, from the planets ---

(Q. And our Earth, from the etheric region of our Earth? Answer: They must pass through the etheric region of your Earth, of course, and to do so must have the permission of the Etherians. Each comes from its own particular rate of vibration which is an unseen pattern of the seen body.

(Q. So, although it is not correct to say that some of

the craft come from Mars, it is correct to say that some of
them come from the etheric duplicate of Mars? Answer: Yes,
that is correct.

(Q. Do they come from all the planets of our system?
Answer: Yes, they come very readily. These craft have often
crossed what you call the Milky Way.

(Q. That means the distances they travel are thousands of
light years -- how can that be? Answer: I think my honorable
colleague Rama Ka Lo tried to point out that these craft are
not what may be termed a solid. Their solidity is formed according to where they are going, what their mission is, and the
particular body in the heavens which they are approaching. As
they come into the sphere of attraction of that body, they have
to make their vibration conform to that of the body.

(Q. Yes, small particles weighing very little on one
planet might weigh a ton on another --

(Q. May I ask something else about these 'ether ships'?
Suppose one of these crafts leaves, say, Arcturus or Orion and
transits into our etheric -- what is it that passes? It is
not any stuff that we know of.

Most assuredly not. It is matter so formed that its,
shall I say behaviorism, its motion pattern can be and is
driven at the speed of light, and beyond. Light is not the
fastest thing. You say light travels at 186,000 miles per
second; add 500 to that and you will have it yet closer. Yet,
under the direction of the -- for the want of another word --
operative force of mind, here and there does not exist. 186,000
miles, and then I say 500 more a second! Doesn't that prove it
is an ever-continuing now? Can anyone conceive of such speed,
really? But still you lay down a law, and all your people
learn that law. Of course, you must have a theory of some
kind -- but to be dogmatic, as some of your scientists are,
about any law shows lack of intelligence on the part of that
scientist. Sir, if there was nobody here and nobody there and
this was a vast void, where would here and there be?

Ramon Natalli (cont'd)

- 1948 -

The phenomena of the 'flying discs' will continue and

probably increase. And no doubt there will be some of your
bold and devoted pilots who will pursue these phantoms of the
skies -- very foolishly, of course.

(---Question).-- No, I have not heard the story of the
flying man.

(---Q.). --- No, we do not change our interpretation of
the 'discs' as we first gave it to you. They do come from the
Etheric world. That does not mean my plane, or any world of
spirits who have lived on your earth, and it does not mean any
planet of your solar system. The etheric world of their origin
interpenetrates with your own.

When we resume our meetings I shall speak more at length
on materialization, which consists in bringing together particles of dense matter by the use of thought force.

(Q. You are suggesting that the 'discs' have their first
material existence on our side, that the etheric prototype of
them is only a thought-form, and that this thought-form acts
to bring them into being in dense matter on our plane of perception?

That is exactly what I am suggesting.

Ramon Natalli (cont'd)

- 1953 -

(Concerning the "little men" observed at the Brush Creek
'disc' landings (and elsewhere. See "Round Robin" IX-2, last
3 pages.):

"The universe swarms with life of many kinds. Some planets
have inhabitants much like yourselves, but on others they differ much in size, weight, density, and other characteristics.
There are giants and pigmies and all sizes between. Among your
sky visitors there are some who come from planets and others
who come from space. (By 'space' the communicator does not
mean vacuity, but rather the enormously dense ethers which
equate with space.)

It is my belief that by 1955 you will be able to land a
rocket on the moon. The conquest of the moon is your next
great project - and it behooves you to make it successful. Its

seisure by another power would mean its domination of the planet - (our Earth.) In landing human beings on the moon there are
two main problems: (a) That of protection from cosmic radiation, (b) That of propulsion.

It would take at least 15 feet of lead to protect you from
the cosmic rays. These would not be immediately fatal, but
life would be very short afterward - five or ten years, perhaps. - Cancer-like growths would appear throughout the body.
But such a heavy lead shield would be impracticable. So, you
cannot use any material you now have - or as you now have it.
But you will find a way to align the atoms and molecules. I
think this will be done by means of powerful electrical impulses or jolts. In the web of energy so created the magnetic
fields will not merge - i.e., the object so shielded will be
weightless. And the great density of the shield will protect
from the cosmic rays. There will be no limit to the speed of
such a weightless object.

The first propulsion used by you will be atomic. But there
is a way to utilize the vibratory rates of the ethers, by a kind
of resonance or harmonics. The people of the 'Discs' could
teach you all these things.

There is so much apprehension among you already, I do not
want to add to it.* . . . . Well, I shall say that your world,
your planet as a whole will suffer a great earthquake. This
will be an ether-quake in its origin. There will be a kind of
disruption of the magnetic or etheric fields. The sky will
seem filled with fire. Great land masses will be displaced;
there will be huge inundations . . . . this will come in a few
years - it will not be many years. More than this I am told I
should not say."

-- (* The last paragraph above was given by Natalli only
under rather insistent questioning.)

Arakashi, Control

- 1950 -

"Your conventional physics has led man to believe that
three dimensional form is real and substantial. But your more
learned physicist will tell you that a physical-chemical object
is rarefied to the point of being ninety per cent space, or what
is known as nothingness, and that that which is called space or
the ether is extremely more dense than any known substance. The
reason for this seems to lie in the fact that no two atoms of
which form is made touch one another, and that, relatively speaking, their distances from one another can be compared with those
separating your heavenly bodies. And that which holds them together or drives them farther apart is called the field of attraction and repulsion, or positive and negative poles. Now,
you can take a bar of iron which may seem real and very solid
to your eyes and sense of touch, but which is as porous as a
piece of sponge, and if you heat this bar, you will find it will
at first start to bend and then to run like water. Why? Simply because heat steps up the vibratory rate of its molecules,
thus creating a greater negative field than existed in it while
cold. This drives the molecules farther apart. Now, while you
have changed the form called a "bar" of iron, you have not in
any way changed the substance called iron because it has become
liquid. You may change it all into vapor but it will still remain "iron" vapor. Now all this latter is well-known even by
the schoolboy; I wish only to make clear that a human body contains all the known elements; and the mind in deep meditation
knows how, with the aid of breath and the kundalini forces, to
segregate the necessary chemicals from the body and project
them into the thought-form mold, thereby creating a three-
dimensional object.

- - - - - - - - - - -

"If your men of science hope to understand more clearly the
phenomena of life, they will have to come sooner or later to
the realization that this thing which we call 'space-time' is
not in its true nature an objective over-all element, but a very
subjective personified activity that is projected from the self
in compact, extremely minute impulses. On the gross earth plane
these impulses are what you call chemical particles - called
this simply because the nuclear structure of these impulses can
be so arranged as to form what you think of as matter - however,

only the kind that is suited for your three-dimensional way of
thinking. But deep within the gross matter field there lies a
more subtle field known as the etheric plane. It is from this
next higher vibratory rate that solidified matter draws its
energy that keeps it functioning in the physical world. When
a physical body of any kind starts to deteriorate and go through
the state you call "death", it is because the channels through
which it absorbs this etheric energy have failed, for one cause
or another. The energy-matter that went to make up that particular body will go through many forms before it again flows back
into its original state of formless matter.

"All that man sees is matter in motion, and then almost
always only one phase of it.

"When seemingly strange phenomena, such as odd-looking aircraft and countless other things come to your notice, you can
be assured that it is one form of matter merging with another
that has an affinity or strong pull of attraction for it. Sometimes the force of attraction is so great that the speed at which
they meet causes them to do what you call explode. An explosion is but one of the many ways that one dimension has of
merging with another by sudden and violent breakdown, or deterioration, and almost instant regrouping to form new substance."

RAMA-KA-LO, Control

- 1950 -

Last week we were speaking about the 'flying discs' -- I
should like to continue. I want to say that traction, or what
would be termed the pressure from the outer to the inner, or as
with the wheels on a road, is created by the magnetic field
they throw off - that is thrown off by the bodies of these
discs. This is true of all of them, including that which you
call a fireball.

(Q. These discs as we see them are what we call materialized. Do they operate or have existence as materialized objects outside our atmosphere? Answer: Yes, they do.

(Q. In that case, is there a different form of propulsion? Answer: No -- lower and higher rates of the same.

(Q. The propulsion then, is not secured by traction on
the gases of the atmosphere, but on the ether?

According to the condition they enter into. Now, atoms
are not single atoms; it is better to say a field, or a pattern, or a wave, or a surface behaviorism. There is always
surface. Going into the higher ethers or lokas there is a denser field; coming into your world atmosphere, the density grows
less and less. Your world is one of the least dense.

(Q. These craft, then, could be used by the Etherians for
interplanetary flight? Answer: Yes, most assuredly -- and
they have been so used in all of what you call time, ever since
matter on your plane or consciousness came into being.

(Q. This implies an acceleration of the vibratory rates
of molecules and atoms; how is this increase in vibratory rates
effected?

Perhaps I can put it into words that will be understandable -- I do not know. Not that you would not understand, but
I am, as you are aware, working with a physical brain that knows
nothing of such things -- but I shall try. To begin, the radiation out of which these things are built is brought about by
mind activity. It is based on the same order as what is called
in the spiritualistic world teleportation.

Teleportation always brings about either extreme heat or cold.
In bringing these manifestations into your world, heat is first
used. After the body becomes dense to your density -- what you
call density -- it starts throwing off heat radiations, heat
energy at a terrific rate of speed. This heat strikes at the
hydrogen and oxygen atoms around the object, creating what may
be called a form of combustion. This combustion brings down
the temperature of the object even as it is climbing again.
This creates a magnetic field around the object, a traction for
it, a road for it.

(Q. It seems possible that if part of an object is suddenly raised to a very high temperature, there would be a
thrust or back-kick against the unheated part. Our Associate,
John Hilliard, calculates that a steel bar one foot long, one-
fourth inch in diameter, heated to 1,000 degrees three million
times a second, if the stretch could be made uni-directional
would take off at about 1,200 miles an hour -- but I take it
that is not what you are talking about. You are speaking of
an external thrust, are you not?

External in a way, because the heated object acts as both
a magnet and a repeller. Sir, it is extremely difficult for
me to put it into words ---

(Q. Is there a heat wave which passes over the exterior
of the disc?

Yes, over the entire surface of the disc is this heat-
wave. I wonder if any of you have noticed the intense glow
around these objects? Some of them reach what you call white
heat. Now, this is heated and cooled at an extremely high rate
of speed. We will need the quantum theory to explain this.

(Q. This "heat-wave" does not affect the interior of the
discs and the people in them? Answer; No, it does not.

(Q. Is it a pick-up-and-lay-down motion, like that of a
caterpillar or inchworm? Answer: Yes, the expansion and
contraction at quantum rates.

(Q. Let me quote a little more of what Associate Hilliard says, 'It's a pick-up and lay-down process in which the
whole substance of the driving mechanism literally flows forward.' I imagine the material of which the driving unit is
comprised (it may be a bar or the skin of the ship) has a

peculiar property which could be called localized heat trans-
fer. If it is heated and cooled rapidly on one end, the hot
and cold spots will travel along the bar. The process is not
so much molecular as it is a space-time process. Heat, light,
etc., are waves or vibrations in the absolute ether, so to
speak. That is infinite, so there is no 'where' in it. In
effect, the waves in the bar stand still; the illusory shape or
etheric substance flows along them by the process, in a molecular sense. And the luminous effect is the radiant discharge
at the end, where the shape slips off the wave form.*

RAMA-KA-LO: Good! That is excellent! I am fascinated
by the explanation. I cannot do well with this boy's brain,
because he knows nothing at all of such things.

(Q. Could we use such a method of propulsion?

I think so -- but in the present state of the world the
cost would be far too great -- far beyond the profits gained --
to produce that kind of heat and to be able to have the kind
of material that would stand up under such heat. It would have
to be an exceedingly tenuous material, and I do not know of
any such in the world today ..... Yes, it would be a synthetic
material.

(Q. What would be the most profitable line of inquiry
for our physicists to pursue in this connection?

The effort to understand what the etheric is, apart from
what are called gases. That would be the first approach -- to
be able to understand this unseen space around you. Also to
be able to understand what is called molecular motion. I do
not think that even your most advanced scientists today understand molecular motion.

(Q. Do you find molecular motion in the ether? Answer:
Yes, it applies to etheric motion. You cannot go anywhere
without finding molecular motion.

(Q. Is all substance on your plane particulate? Answer:
Yes, I know of no such thing as a homogeneous medium on any
plane.

- - - - - -

*NOTE: This concept was developed by Assoc. John A. Hilliard
(Engineer). See The Ethership Mystery, by Meade Layne, pg. 17 f.

(Recent Communications - the Voice of the Yada)

You have asked me this question: Since the 'crossing of space' - of distances measured in terms of light years, is impracticable even at the speed of light, yet the Kareetas or Discs are said to come (some of them) even from beyond the galaxies - what expression can be used to indicate this crossing?

I reply, that the only word I can suggest is emergence. It is used by you in philosophy, and I think in your science also. Consider this set of ivory balls, one within another, within another - ten in all. Each is free to move within another and outside of another. Let us say there is no space at all between them (and indeed there is no such thing as unoccupied space). Now, on each ball there are corresponding points. Any point, that is, any place, space-time place on, say, the outside ball (shall we call it your earth-world?) has a point corresponding to it on its inside, and also on the outside of the second ball - and so on through all the concentric or nested balls. Now, that which IS on the surface of any one ball may emerge on any of the others, without being hindered by any 'crossing of space'. If there is no crossing of space, then the factor of time has no meaning. This illustration, like all others, is of course inadequate, yet it may be helpful.

The 'materialization' of entities in your world is of the nature of an emergence.

(As will be noted later, emergence may also be described as a conversion of energy or a change of vibratory rates. Fortean "falls" are to be accounted for in similar manner. If the vibratory rate of etheric matter is slowed down, it becomes visible and tangible. This would be 'materialization' from our point of view, but a dematerialization from the etheric viewpoint). ml.

You also asked: What does the visitation of the Discs portend? I would say it portends in greatest part the expansion of your sun into a super-nova. The under-strata of the earth are getting hotter, due to an increasing cosmic radiation. More and more of this is passing through the ionosphere. It affects a mutation in the chemistry of the earth and a kind of crystallization of the surface. Huge hollows are formed and the brittle outer crust collapses into them. These physical effects and chemical alterations are being studied by the Space People, and for this reason they are often seen gathering samples of soil and water."

(A question to the Control: Is the future of our planet really known on your plane of existence? Answer: Yes.

(Q. An eminent occultist has recently said, that an 'incredible interplanetary debacle' is in the making. Answer: Yes, I would go along with that.

(Q. Would you say that this event is still remote? Answer: Some things we are not allowed to say and you know that this is one of them. Please excuse me from answering).

(Those who object that the foregoing dislocates both the scientific and occult 'time-schemes' of evolutionary processes fail to allow for the acceleration, which is not a constant and is unpredictable). ml

(The Yada): All this earth talk about the Discs! The mere existence of these objects is nothing new or remarkable. Man has been flying for many centuries in one way or another. But earth people cannot be given the secret of building these objects right away, because if it fell into the hands of any one government it would make war inevitable - though it is, anyway.

Yes, the Canadian scientists know a way of operating a disc-shaped craft, but not as it is done by the Space People - there is almost no comparison. The substances in the space disc are not the same as the groupings you have on your earth. The molecular structure is entirely different - the electronic fields are different. The linking together of molecules (in the disc material) is of such tensile strength that no force known to you can break them apart or cause a cut or break in the substance. . .

The particles that make up the ethers can be thought of as sub-atomic matter, and as we 'sub' lower than that we go out of existence so far as the world of measureable matter is concerned. The ether is 'there' whether for a purpose or not. There is no such thing as 'nothingness' - it is a word, a sound, not even an idea . . . Truthfully, the atom has never been smashed; only a piece of it has been blown away, or thrown away, which is the outer shell, or one of the outer shells. Should

you ever truly break up the atom you would not only turn it
off into another, but you would turn your whole solar system
into a super-solar. The whole system would become nothing but
light radiation, millions of times brighter than your sun.

Concerning the Beings who operate (some of) the aeroforms:
they are not as horrible in their nature as the appearance of
some of them might lead you to believe. It is true that many
of them are not of man form, and being of a much higher menta-
tion they do not possess your emotional responses. They are no
more likely to react to your ideas of good and evil, than you
would to the ideas of an ant or a cockroach. Nevertheless
these beings have no evil intent - for if so they could have
taken over or destroyed the earth aeons ago.

(At this writing, Dec. 7, '53, some disquiet has been
caused by statements purporting to come from the Space People
themselves concerning their "horrible" appearance. It is
also said that the space-craft now overhead are literally
numbered in the millions, and that some kind of action of a
'regulatory' nature is to be expected from them. This is derived from alleged communications from the Aeroforms - which
nevertheless can be accepted pro tem. as valid. By the time
this ms. is published many such questions may be cleared up.
ml)

It is true that the Ethereans have in the past taken large
groups as well as single individuals from the earth and placed
them on other bodies in space, both in and outside of your solar
system, and it is likely they will continue to do this from
time to time. They have also on occasion used human beings for
experimental purposes, much as your men of science do with animals. In any case you have no grounds for moral reproaches
against the Etherean peoples.

(The numerous alleged cases of persons, animals and objects being "taken", visibly and otherwise, now begin to
appear half-way intelligible - though of course not to text-
book science. Teleportation in its narrower sense, as well as
the dissolution of object in 'atomic whirls' or warps will
have to be reckoned with by the science of the near future. ml)

As to the question: Why do space beings need to use the
disc craft and other forms, if they are dwellers in space? Why
can they not move about without a machine of any kind? This
is best answered by another question. Man himself is a space

being; why does he find it necessary to create a form to move about in? Men and Ethereans alike are purely mental beings and are everywhere in consciousness, which is space - but the phenomena of life require form building. All forms are made up of varying degrees of universal life energy and are manifestations of it. When the Ethereans desire you to know of their presence they must create form, so that you can become aware of them through the measuring rods called the senses of the body.

Earth man need have no fear of these beings, unless he attacks them or becomes too inquisitive - in which case it is likely they will retaliate in like manner.

WHAT DO THE DISCS
PORTEND? - By Yada di Shi'Ite. (1953) It is about two and a quarter billion years since man made his first attempt to live on the earth - and about seven billion years since the formation of the primaeval vortex from which the earth arose. Throughout all this enormous period of time (by your measurements) the people of the Discs, in their craft which we call KAREETAS, have been making periodic visits to the earth and studying its nature and action.

All races of men have seen them. Five hundred thousand years ago they were well known to the dwellers in YU, the civilization of the Himalayas.

What does their present coming portend? The universe, the whole Cosmos is expanding. It is like an explosion of the Cosmos. You know that there are dwarf stars, and also that there are Super-Novas. Now, these pass one into the other; each can become the other. This is also true of the Island Universes, which can and do change back and forth. This is the play of atomic energy, of magnetism, of attraction and repulsion. All the stars, the Suns, are in effect huge dynamos . .

These Discs you are asking about - they do NOT belong to the world of three-dimensional matter. They come out of other and far greater densities. They come out of worlds of substance a hundred thousand times more dense than the matter which you perceive by your senses.

The
Rolf   Telano
Communications

(Dictated to BSR Associate R. T.)

THE FLYING SAUCERS

by Rolf Telano, Tk. Com.

1.   There are very ancient laws which declare all intelligent entities, on every planet and plane, and of whatever form,
to be brothers; and to make each responsible for his brother's
welfare. Under this law, the higher races assume the obligation of aiding the material, mental, moral, and scientific
development of all lesser races with whom they come in contact.
The Adamic races of this planet have been under observation by,
and have been receiving aid from, various of these higher races
ever since their beginnings. Some members of their guardian
races have been incarnated among them. Others have come here
from other places, using for transport various craft which are
now popularly, but incorrectly, grouped under the designation
of "flying saucers".

2.   Just prior to World War II, it was noted that certain
sinister forces were gaining considerable influence, and were
likely to create a very dangerous unbalance between scientific
and ethical progress. Scientific knowledge with a high potential of harm was being revealed and pushed rapidly forward before moral development had advanced to a point where such
knowledge could be popularly employed. Observation and other
activities were sharply stepped up to counter this trend.

3.   An even greater increase in activity was made with the
premature discovery of nuclear fission, which represents a
very great menace to all entities on all planes, and "flying
saucers" began to be seen much more frequently than before.
The results of the present uncontrolled heavy metals atomic
explosions, while very annoying, are not particularly dangerous except from the standpoint of atmospheric contamination.
It is possible, however, to employ methods which will react
with certain constituents of this planet, and thus cause its
destruction. The present band of asteroids between Mars and
Jupiter are the remains of a former planet which was destroyed
by this means. The result was catastrophic on all planets and
planes. This particular formula has not yet been discovered
on your planet, and it has been determined that it shall not
be developed.

4.   Contrary to the dire warnings of certain cults and certain astral dwellers, however, there is no desire or intention

of destroying your planet. Neither is there any wish or intent
to depopulate it. Not only is killing forbidden by laws, but
also it is fully recognized that the discarnation of an unde-
sirable entity affords only temporary relief at best, and may
ultimately aggravate the problem. Once they have been re-
oriented on another plane, they have even greater powers than
before and hence, greater power for harm. Any individual dis-
carnations of your people will be only as a last desperate
temporary resort, after all other means have failed. Remember
always that our aim is to aid you, not to harm you.

5.   The present situation might well be analogized by saying
that, when a child reaches a certain age, it must be taught to
employ such useful aids as fire and sharp-edged tools. It must
be watched, however, and perhaps at times even forcibly re-
strained, to prevent it, in its ignorance, from cutting its
own throat or burning the house down. At the moment, the child
has just discovered some things far beyond its ability to understand or safely use. The situation is further complicated by
the fact that some of its more demonic playmates are urging it
to use its newfound knowledge in particularly dangerous ways.
These consist both of entities on the lower astral, and persons
of low intelligence who inhabit the cavern homes of the ancient
Elder Races, and have use of electronic apparatus which was
abandoned there.

6.   It is clearly recognized that the only safe solution for
all concerned is education which will raise the mass intelligence and ethical level of the Adamic races. Restraints cannot be permanently effective, for some will eventually evade
them. Taboos against the use of the things which have been
prematurely learned are worse than useless. Previous experience indicates that, due to some psychological perversity of
the Adamic races, this tends merely to glamorize the forbidden
thing, and make them more determined than ever to do it. Even
temporary restraints can be employed only with great discretion. One learns primarily by their own experience and error.
These educational errors must be permitted, and restraints
should be used only when they threaten to become major trage-
dies.

7.   In the final analysis, no one can "teach" another. One
can merely place information before another, in proper sequence
and in accord with the student's mental capacity and understanding, and then, by various psychological stratagems, attempt
to secure its acceptance as fact. Fear is a powerful stimulus,

and frequently used to channel thought into some desired field.
It too must be used with very great discretion. If a fear is
permitted to become too widespread, or too intense, then the
fearful ones may, by the unconscious use of the laws of thought,
create the very thing which they fear. Some news suppressions
have been the result of stupidity and/or lack of understanding
on the part of your scientists and public officials. Others
have been directed in order to reduce some fear which was getting out of control.

8.   The task of your guardian races is threefold. First and
foremost is to accelerate the spiritual awakening, and the resulting ethical and moral development of the Adamic races.
Second is to closely watch their scientific progress, aiding
that which is beneficial, retarding that which is detrimental,
and temporarily halting that which is disastrous. Third is to
watch the evil influences which may prompt some to take harmful
actions. Interference with these influences will come only if
they threaten to cause very great harm. The Adamic races must
learn to recognize and resist these influences on their own behalf. To this end, they must be permitted to make errors in
judgment in these matters, and to suffer the natural consequenc-
es thereof, that they may learn by their own unpleasant experiences.

9.   These three different tasks are being handled by three
different groups, each of which ordinarily restrict their activities to their own particular task. They work in close harmony
and cooperation, however, and will promptly aid one another if
the need arises. Each also receives valuable aid from many
different groups and individuals on many different planes, including some of the more advanced thinkers of your own plane.
These latter, either knowingly or unknowingly, often are of great
assistance as the "eyes" and "hands" of those from other planes
who cannot work directly on this one.

10.   Since the ethical and moral phases of the task involve
the use of the mental sciences, they are directed by those who
are the recognized masters of these sciences, namely: The
Etheric Atlans and Lemuians. Both of these formerly dwelt on
the material (a) plane of your planet, and are now on the
etheric counterpart of your planet. On rare occasions they may
use some form of mechanical transport, but usually function by
non-mechanical means. Most of the "flying saucers" seen by you
belong to others.

11.   The scientific phases are in the hands of the Etheric Nors, specifically a sub-branch known as the "Viknors". They are the recognized masters of the physical sciences, and for many ages past it has been the custom of the other races to call upon them for aid in scientific matters. One group of them also formerly inhabited the material plane of your planet, but for a much shorter period of time than the other two races. They are now on Mars and Venus Etheria, with the greater part of those who are engaged in the present operations coming from the latter place. Most of the "flying saucers" are operated by them.

12.   The third phase, that of coping with the evil influences, is handled by a mixed group. Actual direction is in the hands of the Lemuians, with the Nors functioning when anything of a mechanical nature is involved. Much work is also done by the more advanced groups in the caverns, and by groups on the various astral planes.

13.   Effective observation and action on any plane can be accomplished only on that plane. Thus the flying saucers of the Venusian Nors must be capable of both inter-planetary and inter-plane travel. They must be brought here from Venus, and converted to the vibrational level of this plane. Any of the various types of craft which you have seen could be transported here individually, if desired. Any of them could also be converted to your vibrational frequency individually, either by the use of their own mechanism, or by external influences. As a matter of operational convenience, however, they are usually brought here in large numbers on a carrier craft. These carriers, by the use of their own mechanism, can teleport themselves to this planet, and simultaneously convert to the desired vibrational level. They remain high above the surface of your planet, in order to prevent detection, and act as a base and coordinating center for their smaller fliers.

14.   In the teleportation method of transportation, the craft and everything on it are converted into pure energy, which is reconverted into its original form at the desired point an almost immeasurable instant later. The control is very delicate, and it is very difficult to exactly place the craft when working from a mobile control. Due to very slight errors, several carriers have been reconverted quite close to the surface of your planet, and it is believed that at least one of these was observed from the surface. To avoid such incidents in the future, the reconversion point is now a considerable distance from your

planet, and the carrier then comes in to the desired altitude
by what you would term "normal space flight".

15. There are several types of carriers, but the only one
so far used in the present operations is known as the "Voku"
class (b). It is about 7,000 feet long, and about 500 feet in
diameter. It normally carries a crew of about 2,500, including the technicians and the pilots of the smaller fliers. They
can use several different types of propulsion, according to circumstances. They are heavily armed.

16. The smaller fliers use several different types of propulsion. A form of jet propulsion, although very ancient, is
still extensively used. A very small "dis" ray, playing upon
a stream of fuel in a closed chamber, atomically disintegrates
it. The usual fuel is air, which is collected in scoops by
the forward motion of the craft, and automatically compressed
to injection pressure. Other fuels, including metals, can be
used in airless locations. The end products of the process are
radio-active, and can be detected by means of usual test apparatus. Since none of the heavy metals group is ever used
for fuel, however, the radioactivity is very short-lived, and
does not cause any permanent atmospheric contamination.

17. Electro-magnetic drive operates by cutting the natural
magnetic lines of force produced by a planetary body, and can
be used only relatively near the surface of some planet. When
used at low altitudes, it has the effect of "blanking out"
radio apparatus, and causing variations in magnetic compasses
and other magnetic apparatus in the vicinity.

18. "Primary drive" is a true space drive and, although it
can be used on a planet, it is ordinarily used only when it is
desired to travel at a very high rate of speed for a long distance. Control mechanism on the craft is placed in snychron-
ous frequency with the universal energy flows which exist in
all space, but slightly out of phase with them. Either "lag-
ging" or "leading" phase can be used, depending upon whether
it is desired to travel with the flows, or against them. The
speed depends on the degree of phase angle which, in turn, depends on the amount of "shading power" which the control apparatus can apply. The maximum potential speed is never real-
ized, since practical navigation and control problems usually
limit the top usable speed to about 27,000 miles per hour. A
few exceptionally skilled pilots have exceeded this.

19.   In addition to the three types of propulsion listed,
all craft have means of hovering motionless when desired. One
piece of apparatus produces a cone-shaped electrical field
which diverts the flow of "gravity" around the craft; much as
an umbrella diverts rain, thus cancelling most of the "weight".
Another produces a downward electron beam jet which compensates
for the slight remaining "weight". It is quite common to use
the diversion field while in flight, in order to reduce the
effective mass of the craft, thus making it more maneuverable
and reducing the amount of power required to maintain flight.
This field will, under certain conditions, produce a corona discharge which will give the craft the appearance of being surrounded by a luminous or fiery envelope. A similar corona effect is also quite common on craft using the electro-magnetic
form of propulsion.

20.   The Viknors have, to date, used seven different types
of fliers:
        (1). "Suza" class. These are "doughnut" shaped, about 125
feet outside diameter, with a "hole" about 25 feet in diameter,
and about 30 feet thick. They are sometimes referred to as
"flying laboratories", because of the large amount of test
equipment which they carry. They are an observation craft, and
used only when very involved technical observations are required. Normal crew: 50. Electro-magnetic drive.
        (2). "Tonton" class. Cigar-shaped, about 100 feet long
by 25 feet maximum diameter. Primarily an escort and fighter
craft. Used only if circumstances require protection for the
other craft. Normal crew: 20. Uses both jet and primary
drive.
        (3). "Fakle" type. Spherical, about 100 feet in diam-
eter. A transport craft, used to carry both passengers and
cargo. Normal crew: 25 or 30. Electro-magnetic drive.
        (4). "Olon" type. Crescent or rubber heel shaped, about
45 feet across by 18 feet thick. Reconnaissance craft. Normal crew: 5. Uses jet drive, one jet being placed in a universal mounting at each of the points of the crescent. Control
is by changing the direction of these jets; no external control
surfaces being used. This is a very ancient type of flier, but
well suited to the requirements of the present task and, therefore, the type most frequently seen.
        (5). "Oloner" type. Similar in shape and construction
to the "Olon" type, but much smaller, being only about 14 feet
across. A "single place" flier, but can carry two when required.

(6). "Pomid" type. Spherical, about 5 or 6 feet in diameter. Robot and remote controlled from some other craft. Used for visual observation where larger craft would attract too much attention. Electro-magnetic drive.

(7). "Pomider" type. A smaller version of the "Pomid", being only about one foot in diameter. Frequently mistaken for a "fireball".

21.   Aside from the Viknor craft described, various other types are seen at very infrequent intervals. Some groups on your planet and plane have found and re-activated very ancient fliers which were left here by the old "Elder Races". These are mostly predecessors of the "Olon" class. Visitors from other solar systems occasionally come to this one for various purposes. If their purpose is not malicious, they are permitted to proceed. Otherwise they are usually intercepted and turned back in the outer limits of this solar system.

22.   The craft most deserving of the name "flying saucers" were brought to this planet in 1949 by a midget race from your moon (c). These were slightly less than 100 feet in diameter, but much of this area was areo-dynamic surface, the actual cabin being only about 16 feet in diameter. They used an electro-magnetic, or "earth induction" drive, but different in construction than that used by the Nor craft. It was their first interplanetary flight, and their purpose was peaceable exploration. They became stranded here, without base or supervisory control, when the carrier craft became disabled. The small fliers were unable to return to Luna, because they were incapable of space flight.

23.   One of the Lunar fliers was shot down over northern Mexico by the over-anxious pilot of a Nor patrol craft, when it failed to respond to signals, or otherwise identify itself. Several others were caused to crash by radar, to which they were particularly susceptible because of insufficient shielding of their drive and control apparatus. As soon as it became apparent that the return of their carrier would be indefinitely delayed, and that the craft and pilots were unable to cope with conditions on this planet, they were rounded up and returned to Luna by a Viknor carrier. Of the original 37 fliers, 26 were safely returned to their home base. Eight are known to have crashed. It is assumed that the remaining 3 went down unnoticed.

- - - - - - - - - - - -

Note (a). The word "material" is used as a matter of convenience to indicate your particular vibrational plane. It is,
of course, technically incorrect, since all other planes are
also "material", usually more so than this one, but merely on
a different frequency.

Note (b). The class names of the various craft listed are the
nearest English spellings of the actual phonetic names.

Note (c). "The atmosphere and water on Luna and, consequent-
ly, the life, is mainly concentrated on the far side, which
is never seen from your planet. The condition is analogous
to a bucket of water being whirled at the end of a rope, with
the water being held at the far end by the action of centrif-
ugal force. Expeditions have come to the near side to attempt
to signal Earth on several occasions. In several instances the
signals were seen by your astronomers, but were ignored because of their firm belief that Luna was lifeless."

- Rolf Telano.

NOTE:
    The Intermediary or 'Receiver' of the foregoing material,
'Rolf Telano', is an electronics engineer by profession and a
resident of the Middle West. He has never publicized or ex-
ploited his psychic gifts. The above material was received by
a kind of inner dictation or clairaudience, with partial control of the hands on the typewriter. I have found no reason,
during my near-decade of contact with him, to question his
integrity or the authentic nature of the psychism involved.
                                                    M.L.

COMMENTS OF THE YADA DI SHI'ITE

(Mark Probert Trance Control)

On January 24, 1952, the document received through 'Rolf Telano', and printed on preceding pages, was read to the Tibetan control Yada di Shi'Ite, Mark Probert being in deep trance at the time. The object, of course, was to obtain the comments, either pro or contra, of this highly respected communicator, with whom we have been in almost weekly contact for nearly five years. Since there has always been a basic agreement among the fifteen communicators of this group, we feel reasonably certain that statements by the Yada have the support of other members of the group as well. We quote the substance of his comments only:

Comment by   'I see no reason why this communication from
the Yada: your Associate known as Rolf Telano, should not
                  be made public, since a few will profit by it
                  and others will not be harmed. It should, how-
                  ever, be presented with the utmost circumspec-
                  tion.

'First of all, your readers should bear in mind that the situation and events with which the R.T. communication deals are highly complex and relate not only to your planet but in various ways to the entire solar system. Precise and exact statements concerning matters of such magnitude are almost impossible and should be taken with reserve - not as being wrong, but as necessarily inadequate.

'Approaching with this attitude of mind, I find no serious errors in the document you have read to me.

'Concerning the "Etheric Atlans and Lemuians ... both of whom formerly dwelt on your planet and are now on the etheric counterpart of your planet" (Para. 10). Do not take this as implying that entire races enter the etheric directly after leaving earth life. But many individuals can and do enter the etheric worlds, according to their personal status and destiny. The statement about the etheric NORS is correct, again with reference to a group.

'I have no knowledge of any construction work in the caverns or of any craft issuing from that source.' (Para. 12). (Note: this is the sole point on which the Yada showed pronounced skepticism. M.L.)

'The data about the carrier craft is essentially correct (Para. 13-15). And the reconversion mentioned, of these craft, to the vibrational level of your plane, is one important cause of the explosions in the atmosphere and ethers.

'The expression "heavily armed" should not be taken as meaning, against yourselves. -- Yes, it is true that there is something like a policing of your planet and of the entire so-lar system. -- Yes, the statement about 'guardian races', their purposes, duties, and so on, (Para. 1-9) is essentially correct. Your visitors truly wish you well and desire to help and protect you. Is it wise to meet them with fear and with hostility?

'Well, 27,000 miles an hour is not very fast!' (Note: that this speed refers to our vibrational level, not to cross-ing interplanetary distances, which is accomplished by other means. M.L.)

'Concerning the Moon, etc. (Para. 22): There is no race which permanently inhabits the Moon. But the Moon has been used for ages (on its "dark side") as a meeting ground, for scientific work, and for many meetings of occult or secret Orders. Yes, signals have been sent to your earth from the Moon. The incidents described (accidents to the Lunar flight, the help by the Viknor carrier, etc.) actually occurred.

'The huge craft called Kareeta' (Fall of 1946) over San Diego, came from the Moon."

- - - - - - - - - - -

(The following additional material has been received sub-sequent to the Comments by the Yada just quoted. It was given to Associate Rolf Telano, and is by way of reply to inquiries sent him by the BSR Director. The communicator is "Borealis Telano", and she begins by telling her earth friend that --

'These matters are much too complicated to be dealt with on a part-time basis. You had best stick to your own job and not bother your head too much with such affairs. However...'

Borealis Telano

(a) The words "planes", "Earthians", "Etherians" and so on, are rather ill-advised although they are occasionally used as a matter of convenience. In the minds of most people, however, they build up too much of a picture of definite places, with fixed boundaries - and perhaps even a customs and immigration service.

(b) All planes are actually one. There is merely a continuously increasing vibrational frequency, beginning with the "sub-physical" and rising through the "physical", "Astral", and "Etheric" to the final and original Source. Entities simply gravitate to some particular height on the scale, according to their individual desires and mental abilities. The lower ranges, from and to which the dwellers successively incarnate and discarnate to and from the "physical" are usually called the "Astral" planes. The upper ranges, where such return to the lower physical is rare, are commonly referred to as the "Etherics". All divisions are arbitrary. None can say where the upper Astral stops and the lower Etheric begins. All names and designations are artificial inventions, and have only as much meaning as the individual user assigns to them.

(c) All entities on all planes were probably on the physical of some planet or other, at some time, though it may have been countless eons ago in some cases. Therefore, all are probably former "Earthians" in the strict technical sense. The higher one rises on the vibrational scale, the thinner becomes the cord which binds them to earthy or physical things. Eventually they reach a point where all connection with the "physical" is, for all practical purposes, broken. Their thoughts and interests are along entirely different lines, and they have no desire to return to the physical. There is no actual reason why they could not return, if they wished to do so, and there have been cases where some have done so. Perhaps after a few millions or billions of years one can become bored even on Heavi'n.

(d) The particular group which dictated the "Flying Saucer" report dwelt on the Etheric, but not on the highest levels. The number who incarnate to the physical is very small as compared to the total, and even these volunteer for such incarnation mainly from a sense of obligation rather than any personal preference. Their sole motive is to aid the Adamic races of your planet and plane. They can, to a certain degree, function by merely materializing, or converting to the frequency of your plane. Such requires constant mental effort to maintain the proper vibrational frequency, however, and hampers effective total thought to that degree. Therefore a certain number are actually incarnated into earth-born physical bodies, and live out a normal lifetime.

(e) Aside from their obligations under certain cosmic laws, the groups are tied to the Adamic races by the fact that they created them, and are therefore particularly responsible for them. When these groups first came to the physical plane of your planet, they found that their physical bodies were not entirely to its environment. In an effort to improve the situation they began, by selective breeding and cross-breeding, to develop a better adapted physical body. The final choice was the ancestor race of the present Adamic races, which was a cross between the Elder Races themselves and a certain man-like animal native to your planet. This ancestor animal is now extinct. During experimentation these physical forms were inhabited by the KUIS ("spirits") of some of the lower ones among the Elder Races, and certain animal life forms. This is not recognized by your theologies, but every living thing has a KUI (what you would call "soul" or "spirit"), and these Kuis differ only in the degree of their advancement. They can and do evolve in successive incarnations, and can and do ultimately inhabit physical bodies of human form. It would not be advisable to publicize this statement as it would create too much opposition at present.

(f) The intention to incarnate into the bodies of the Adams was abandoned long before they had been developed to a satisfactory point, because the Elder Races had in the meantime learned how to advance themselves to a more suitable vibrational level. The Adams were left behind in their imperfect state, but the members of the former parent races still recognize a special obligation to aid them in their development".

(end of dictation by Borealis Telano)

On the evening of February 4, 1952, the BSR Director made inquiry of the trance Control LO SUN YAT (a Tibetan), speaking through the mediumship of Mark Probert. The questions referred chiefly to the subject matter of paragraphs c) and d) above, and the substance of the replies was as follows:

LO SUN YAT: Yes, there are such Guardian Races, and their responsibility stems from the facts described. This cross-breeding actually took place, in the dim past, but the race resulting from this union came to an end with Lemuria... The "man-like animal native to your planet" was originally created by the Etheric "colonizers" ... The 'cross' was not a true ancestor race, it was a kind of ancestral pattern resembling man in form. Man originated from a later experiment ....

In one of their experiments to become one with the material
world, some forms that were made resembled the anthropoid apes.
... Yes, there was actual mating between the Etherians and these
earth-animals. "Sons of God mating with daughters of men" - a
fine rhetorical statement but not a pretty thing by any means
- if you could only see what they looked like ... About the
KUIS - these are the "servient spirits" of your Huna. Yes,
they are a kind of fragmentation of a human entity. The Higher
Mind may for various reasons leave the Low Self in control of
the body. Many KUIS are now in human bodies. Very many indeed
in Asia, Africa, India. They possess animal instincts only.
Those who seem to have no aura possess the chemical-radiation
aura only. One may say that the KUIS are the lower or the
lowest part of the mind. They are a dissociated part.

Yes, certainly, there are races of Etheric people who are
not excarnate humans and have never lived on earth. Some of
the "discs" and other sky-craft are truly operated by excarnate earth people, but some are operated by the "true" Etherians. They will be in your skies until there is no more threat
of world-war.... I do not want to appear to speak for them, but
if they have to attack it may well be by great sheets of flame
out of the sky and by great concussions.... Your globe is like
an atom in the cosmos, but every atom has its contacts, its
effects. Perhaps you must be protected from yourselves and
perhaps the solar system must be protected from you.

(end of communication by Lo Sun Yat)

- - - - - - - - - - - - - - - -

CONCERNING THE ROLF TELANO COMMUNICATIONS

A Corrective Memorandum, by Rolf
Telano and the Communicators.

(Some of the most remarkable and instructive material we
have ever received concerning the aeroforms and the entities
using them, has come via our Associate Rolf Telano. R.T. is a
qualified technician or engineer in radio-electronics, and has
never employed his psychic gifts for profit or in a public manner. In October, 1952, he sent us material from which we compiled an 11-page brochure (Release "1-B-52") which had a third
printing in January, 1954. The prefatory page to this states
that the principal thesis was that "the disc-shaped craft are
operated by excarnate humans now living on the Etheric Venus
(not on the astral)".

The trance control Yada Di Shi'Ite advised us that the
brochure could be released "but with the utmost circumspec-
tion". He added that the subject was so complex that any information received by us would be inadequate, though not necessarily wrong. Later, in August, 1952, he stated that "none of
the Discs were operated by excarnate humans". He did not im-
pugn the veracity of Rolf Telano but felt that there was a
misunderstanding somewhere. This acute insight on the part
of the Yada has now been substantiated by the R. T. Communicators themselves, as the following document bears witness.
The whole episode is instructive and profitable, and we are
greatly indebted to the etheric communicators, to the Inner
Circle of the M. P. Controls, and to our Associate Rolf Telano,
whose singular gifts and painstaking accuracy have made this
information available.*

*Note: Release (brochure) "1-B-52" is still available at BSR
Headquarters. It contains six pages from the etheric communi-
cators, comments by the Yada, a letter from Rolf Telano, a
"further note on humans in Etheria", a letter from "Borealis
Telano", and a short commentary by the M.P. Control Lo Sun
Yat. (12 pages, 8½ x 11 - $1.00).

EXCERPTS FROM LETTER - ASSOC. ROLF TELANO to the B.S.R. DIREC-
TOR:

"........ Regarding the 'excarnate humans' -- it would now appear that they did not describe themselves as such but, rather,
that I so described them -- and that the description is in
error. This was partially due to misunderstanding on my part,
and partially due to my incorrect use of certain words in my
article. The corrected version is as follows:

They did not originate on Earth, or on any planet with a
similar vibrational level. They have always been high plane
dwellers. They have never used the word "etheria" in any communication, although I assumed (and still assume) that the
place they describe is what you term "etheria". Their own
name for their dwelling place has always been "heavi'n".

"Heavi", like our "heavy", means "dense". "'N" is the
abbreviation of a source concept. The free translation into
English would be: "A place of great density, from which we
originated." Since great density would also be high vibrational frequency, it would seem to me that this would be
"Etheria", or something very close to it. It seems that the
same places and planes have several different names in some
cases.

They came to Earth before there were any native Earthlings
on it. In fact, they came for the purpose of bringing life,
including human, to Earth, and guiding it until it was able to
shift for itself. To do this, they had to bring themselves to
the Earth-plane level. I regarded this as "incarnating", but
they have since corrected me, and said that it was not an
"incarnation" as the word is used here, since they did not
enter Earth-born bodies. Their bodies were the same high-
plane bodies which they had always had, only converted down to
this level for the time being, much as is done with the Aeroforms at present. The "time being", as I understand it, was
several thousand years, which is a "long time" to us, but only
a brief interlude in their time-concept.

There were a few cases where some of their number actually
left their high-plane bodies for a time, and entered Earth-
born bodies. These were the "surface observers", who lived
among the Earthlings. It seems that it is more difficult for
an isolated individual to maintain himself on this level than

it is for a group. He must constantly exert mental power to keep "tuned in", which diverts considerable mental power away from other uses. In these cases it was <u>formerly</u> the custom to actually incarnate these few.

However, they point out that this did not make him an "Earthling". The material body is not the individual, and the real entity who was temporarily wearing the body would still be a high-plane dweller, and would return to a high-plane body upon his return.

As I said, this was occasionally done <u>formerly</u>. In comparatively recent times ("recent" again in their time concept) they have constructed a mechanism at their Lunar base which transmits a simulated mental ray, which they call the "master pulse wave". This is the proper frequency to convert them to this level or plane. All the Aeroforms, and surface observers, have a simple mechanism which will enable them to "lock in to synchronism" with the master pulse. This will automatically keep them at this vibrational level without any further thought on their part. They can, at any desired time, cut out the mechanism, and assume mental control over their vibrational level.

My contacts corrected me on this point some time ago but, since it required a rather lengthy explanation, and I was rather busy, I did not pass it along. As a matter of fact, I regarded it as a very minor point. Recently, however, I have received some correspondence from people who seem to feel that this is a basic difference, and that it impugns the B.S.R.A. Etherian hypothesis - so I haste to pass it along. As I see it, the corrected explanation is quite compatible, and would tend to confirm the Etherian hypothesis, rather than attack it.

To sum up, they regard themselves as "humans", but apparently in a much broader sense than it is ordinarily used, because they were never Earthians, but have always been high-plane dwellers. To them, a "human" is a being on <u>any</u> plane who employs a thinking and reasoning process similar to our own.

They have also pointed out to me recently that their appearance, in most cases, is not a "materialization" and "de-materialization", in their definition of the words. They regard "materialization" as creating matter from pure energy. Teleportation does actually employ a "dematerialization-materialization" process -- but they regard your term of "emergence" as more correctly describing the process in ordinary cases. That is, they are "there", all the time -- they are quite "solid" all the time (to themselves). They described it with a quite simple analogy, which might be of some use to you in describing it to others:

If you travel from New York to Washington, your reality has ceased to "exist", so far as the New York range of perception is concerned. Yet, you are the same "you" as you have always been, and you are quite "real" to yourself, and to anyone else on the Washington range of perception. It is exactly the same with the Aeroforms, except that, instead of travelling on the horizontal surface, they are travelling up and down the vibrational scale.

Since they have a much wider range of perception than we, it is possible for them to raise their level just slightly above the upper limit of our range, but still stay within their range. Thus they can observe without being observed, if desired. The Aeroforms over Washington, which went out of visual sight, but remained within "sight" of the radar, was an example of this. The radar has a much higher range than our eyes. I would assume that these relatively slow mutations which some have observed might be some Aeroform occupant sort of "fishing around" for this marginal level.

(signed) Associate R. T.

N I N E T E E N P A R A G R A P H S

(Recent Light on the Problem of the U.F.O.)

- and -

Comment on the Same
By Edward S. Schultz, Regional Director B.S.R.A.

THE PARAGRAPHS)
(v. note at end)
  of article):)

1. It is true that a few human beings -
('Earthians') have entered Discs and
other aeroforms and have taken short
rides in them.

2. No Earthian has travelled in an aeroform to distances beyond the
gravitational and magnetic field of the earth. No Earthian has
visited the Moon, Mars, Venus, or any other planet <u>while in his
normal physical body.</u>

3. No Earthian can make an interplanetary or true space flight in
an aeroform <u>while in his normal physical body.</u> Such a flight
would be possible provided his body were reconditioned prior to
entering the aeroform. But further ---

4. This reconditioning would consist in a <u>time-measured</u> dosage of
high frequencies produced by small <u>electronic devices</u> - and -

5. True space flight, even if achieved by a human under the protection mentioned, would result in amnesia and serious physical
disorders.

6. Recurring to "4" supra: An aeroform at rest is enveloped by a
field of <u>supersonic</u> frequencies; and an aeroform in flight gives
off a <u>field of ultra</u>-sonic frequencies.

7. Ultrasonic rates actually convert the aeroform, and the bodies of
all persons inside of them, to waves of light. Etherean beings in
this condition retain full consciousness and full control of their
'ship'. But no normal human can survive this conversion unless previously conditioned by time-measured dosage of high frequencies.
Even if so protected, it is very doubtful whether he could return
to normal earth life, or survive for any considerable length of
time.... The conditioning affects the blood stream and the bone marrow and prevents the blood from "boiling" -- but in the end produces
amnesia and hemorrhage.... The subject conditioned would not necessarily be aware of what was being done.... Ultrasonic frequencies
loosen the cell structure but do not disintegrate the cells.

8. Travelling as a light wave the Etherian is able to control his (light wave) craft by mental energies and by the use of ultrasonic frequencies.

9. The speed of light in free space is without limit. In occupied space (planets and other bodies) light is affected by gravitational pressures. In free space therefore, transition is instantaneous. A change of frequency is equivalent to a change of position or location. (An electron is believed to change its orbit "instantly", i.e., without using time to do so...... Cp. Natalli on the time vacuum. (ml).

10. Ultra-sonic frequencies produced by electronic devices can act as a gravity screen (shield). A resting Disc can cut off the gravity screen (shield). A resting Disc can cut off the gravity pressure from any angle, and will then be thrown off into space by gravity itself - or -

11. When the material of which the craft appears to be made has its vibratory rate raised to ultrasonic frequencies it becomes invisible and intangible ipso facto.

12. When converted as in "11" sup., the craft may remain in situ, translucent, transparent and invisible, tangible or intangible; or it may depart without being perceived.

13. Recurring to "6" sup. Conversion to ultra-sonic frequencies affects all parts of the body at the same instant, and the Etherians experience no ill effects. They can travel as conscious living light waves, or in bodies resembling our own at another frequency.

14. From this point of view ("13") it is possible to describe the aeroforms as the living bodies of etheric entities (as has been done). The 'ship' and its 'crew' alike become light waves or frequencies of the ether; while consciousness continues to abide in the entities - who may be unaware of physical changes in themselves.

15. According to their vibratory rates, the ether ships pass through each other and through other objects, and penetrate the depths of the sea and the 'solidity' of earth. The ultrasonic force field about them will also on occasion destroy aircraft and other objects, with effects resembling those of extremely violent collision. Mantell's plane, and his body, were almost certainly destroyed in this manner.

16. As often pointed out by us heretofore, there is no crossing of space where transit of free space is in question - since the speed of light is then without limit, instantaneous, not requiring time. Light does not "cross space".

17. It is known by experience that resting Discs are often dangerous to touch (v. "6" sup.). It is possible that some persons may be less affected by supersonic frequencies than others; this may account for the selection of certain persons by the Etherians. It is also possible that some such persons are now showing signs of amnesia and other physical and mental deterioration. (These are my own conjectures only. m.l.)

18. Recur to "16", last sentence, <u>Light</u>, etc. There is a gravity time-lag in occupied space, but light and darkness are permanent conditions of the ethers, or frequencies of the ethers - not 'something that is going somewhere'.

19. Persons abducted by the ether-ships are treated by time-measured doses of ultra-sonic frequencies, are usually landed on other planets and suffer amnesia with respect to their earth lives. It is said that they are well treated.

ANALYTICAL COMMENT)
on the 19 Para.,) 1. This appears to more or less corroborate
by Edw. S. Schultz -) the Saucer visit and/or ride stories of
Bethurum and Dan Fry, in terms of physic-
al body adventures, in full, physical cons-
ciousness and within the earth's gravitational and magnetic fields.

2. However, the preconditions in this para.' automatically rule out the widely publicized Saucer rides and planetary visits of another claimant who, by hotly insisting that he made the alleged rides into outer space in his physical body and consciousness; has been pulling the rug out from under himself in more ways than one.

3. This is very logical. However, in re to a space travel adventure and a Saucer contact via a <u>pre-conditioned consciousness</u>, I recall the case cited in "Uranus", of August, 1954, by Chibbett, wherein the visit <u>into</u> a Saucer in flight was made by a woman in hypnotic trance. It remains for someone to report a case of Saucer contact via astral projection.

4. Here, I wonder if such physical body reconditioning could also be done via hypnosis, via certain drugs or Yoga practices. Note the parallel in fire-walking, done via certain Yoga and Huna techni-ques. Some Yogi have lately asserted that the effects of deadly atomic radiations could be entirely overcome or neutralized by such Yoga practices.

5. This would seem to indicate that, even with the physical body pro-tected by proper "reconditioning"; by-product Saucer radiation might have an effect on the Etheric double or even higher vehicles

of human consciousness. There have been several reports of such harmful side effects.

6. Since the terms "Ultrasonic" and "Supersonic" are not synonymous, their true (orthodox) meaning would seem to indicate that the reverse might be true. The possibility of such transposition, in transcription, etc., should be ruled out. If not, the terms probably have meanings outside the realm of atmospheric acoustics, as normally understood.

7. This could be especially true or more understandable if we consider the super-physical properties of the four invisible, to us, Etheric (but still material) grades of matter, which normally make up our physical bodies as well as Saucers tuned in to our physical octave of manifestation, etc.

8. Here we can recall Theosophical and other literature concerned with the properties of our higher octave "mental bodies" and "mental matter". By conversion from physical to "mental matter", Etherians and their craft can travel between galaxies, with a speed far, far beyond the speed of light and.... without the well-known relativistic drawback of infinite mass that physical matter is subject to at speeds equal to that of light.

9. It would seem that, in such "free space", light quanta might partake of the properties of "mental matter". In terms of the higher realities, all matter, on all octaves of manifestation is basically "mental matter", i.e., projected and sustained in the consciousness of the Absolute.

10. Not, I infer, in terms of Ultrasonic frequencies in the atmosphere, but, more likely, in the afore-mentioned four states of Etheric matter, which are just beyond the rarest gases but....still physical.

11. Analogous to the way in which physical matter, made sufficiently radioactive, is transformed into invisible radiations, i.e., a higher frequency of matter, as it were.

12. This means that Etherians have the secret of tuning in on various octaves of matter, in and out of our range of perception, or half way between. In the latter case a Saucer craft would appear to be semi-transparent, as in the reported cases of "jellyfish" appearances.

13. This is covered by and amplifies some of my previous comments, above.

14. Some of our Yogi's are masters of such (frequency conversion)

space travel. For authentic instances of this read the fascinating and inspiring "Autobiography of a Yogi", by P. Yogananda.

15. There is more than ample corroborative evidence of this throughout the realm of the more advanced "Saucer" literature.

16. See comment 8 and 9, above. Mental octaves of frequency transcend all physical barriers and orthodox science notions of cosmic order.

17. This is undoubtedly true. The faculty of Etheric vision, weak or missing in most individuals might make it possible for some to see Saucer phenomena quicker and easier than the majority.

18. Einstein postulated one such important effect of gravitational fields on light, and this was amply proved by direct, astronomical measurement.

19. Etherians have undoubtedly been "pollinating" beautiful planets of remote galaxies in space for ages, with "Adams and Eve samples" of humanity. Thus, when trigger-happy war-mongers do happen to make this planet uninhabitable with an atom bomb war, the Etherians may merely shrug, knowing that the teeming humanities they have planted on so many other spheres in space, are still busy carrying out the Divine evolutionary plan.

(March '56)

NOTE: The "Nineteen Paragraphs" previously appeared in our Clips & Quotes E-11, and was also sent out as a brochure - No. 1-1-6. We of course a-void lengthy reprints of our own material - but in this case the Paragraphs are of great importance - and so too is the Commentary on them by Assoc. E.S.S. This latter, however, will not be intelligible unless the Paragraphs are at hand for easy reference.

We have repeated literally scores of times, in various BSR publications, simplified statements of the "Etheric" or "4-D" interpretation of the Aeroforms (UFO). We will spare our readers further repetition here. If you have use for them, ask for our "Public Information" brochure. We have also explained many times the source from which the Etheric interpretation was derived.

This interpretation has stood the test of time. It was received by us in the fall of 1946, and practically all subsequent phenomena can be subsumed under it. It has been expanded and elaborated somewhat, but none of the basic statements have been abandoned or withdrawn. It is steadily gaining favor among investigators, especially in England - and will do so in this country whenever the word metaphysics comes to be properly used and understood. And let me again make plain, that the "etheric interpretation" is not the invention of any BSR Associate - nor is it cultist or religionistic, but rather a new factual impact of very ancient knowledge. m.l.

From BSRA "Round Robin" of Mar-Apr 1956: issue XI-6

Concepts of the Ether

One of the principal difficulties in trying to make the "4-D" or Etheric interpretation of the aeroforms understandable, is the idee fixee that the ether (aether) is an outmoded hypothesis. The explanation for this attitude, of course, lies in the whole history of the subject since the days of Lodge. But it would be easy to show, by numerous quotations, that the ether is as much a reality and logical necessity today as are protons and electrons. Note the following brief example:

"The real electron, the part that acts, is the surrounding ether which is outside its geometric boundary; and the electron theory is the science of the properties of the ether..." (C. W. Richardson in Electron Theory of Matter).

"It may be found that the ether is, after all, what is fundamental and that electrons and hydrogen nuclei are merely states of strain in the ether". (Bertrand Russell, in A.B.C. of Atoms).

"The foremost men of the age accept the ether, not as a vague dream but as a real entity". (Tydal, in Light & Electricity).

"It is possible that an electron is a kind of disturbance in the ether, most intense at one spot ... It is equally possible that a hydrogen nucleus may be explained in a similar way". (Russell, op. cit.)

Eddington, as is well known, says emphatically that we cannot dispense with the ether, and that in trying to do so we have to attribute properties to the interspaces and represent them by 'a host of symbols'. The phrase 'empty space' is meaningless and the old problem of actic in distans is still unconquered.

Now referring to the explanation we favor, that there is no "crossing of space" measured in light years, by the aeroforms, we refer again to Russell, who remarks that the process by which an electron changes its orbit is inexplicable - since it happens instantaneously contrary to all known physical laws. "Perhaps", (he says) "there is No intervening space..." In like manner the ether ships emerge from one into another frequency, and thereby appear in a different place. There is no 'empty space' to cross, and hence no time required for transit.

- - - - - - - - - -

"V I B R A S O N I C S"

and

Conditions of Space Transit

(NOTE: The term <u>vibrasonics</u> refers to the upper stages of the sound spectrum or harmonic scale, beyond ultra-sonics. The word is coined by R. R. Russell, in his article in <u>Flying Saucer Review</u> (Lon.) for Nov.-Dec., 1955.*

(The following paragraphs are an Addendum to our Brochure 1-1-6 and to other BSR material relative to the phenomena of the aeroforms (UFOs). Mr. Russell's substantial agreement with our Etheric interpretation is the result of his own independent investigation and study).

1. It is true that a few human beings ('Earthians') have entered the Discs and other aeroforms and have taken short rides in them. But no earthian has travelled in an aeroform in free space, or has visited the Moon, Mars, or Venus or any other planet <u>while in his normal physical body</u>.

2. Such flight into free space or within the solar system may be possible in theory at least, provided the physical body be pre-conditioned by a <u>time-measured</u> dosage of high frequencies (ultra-sonic or 'vibrasonic').

3. Persons who have travelled for short distances in the neighborhood of the earth have been exposed to the ultrasonic frequency field which surrounds the craft in flight, and may have been conditioned without their own knowledge.

4. The high frequencies referred to are generated by small electronic devices. Many mechanisms are employed by the Etherians, (as by Earthians) merely as a matter of convenience but not from necessity.

5. True space flight, if achieved by a human even under the protection mentioned, would result in amnesia and serious physical disorders. The conditioning itself affects the blood stream and the bone marrow. Further, the 'subconscious' or unconscious mind of the human is deeply conditioned to all factors of earth life, and will be unable to accept the immense frequency changes, even though the conscious self may give consent.

6. The ultrasonic frequencies convert the aeroform and the bodies of persons inside them, to the frequency of light waves. Under these conditions the Etherians retain full consciousness and full control of their 'ship', but no earth person could survive them, except by such

----

*Pub. at 1 Doughty St., Lon. W.C. 1, Eng. Every other month, $3.50. Recommended.

preconditioning as has been mentioned; and even so it is doubtful that he could return to normal earth life.

7. Etherian craft in free space (or where desired) travel at the speed of light waves, or greater: there is no limit to the 'speed of light' in free space. This 'travel' is a matter of conversion of frequency rates and can be controlled by mind energy and by the use of ultrasonic (electronic) apparatus.
These frequencies can act as a gravity screen or shield. This statement will be verified by earth scientists and it is unnecessary to point out its extreme importance.

8. Conversion to ultra-sonic frequencies affects all parts of the human body at the same instant and the Etherians experience no ill effects. They travel as conscious living light waves where the 'crossing' of inter-stellar distances is concerned. More correctly, there is no transit of space, but only the change of frequency which is equivalent to a change of location.

9. An aeroform at rest is surrounded by a super-sonic field; when in flight it produces an ultra-sonic or vibrasonic field. These craft pass easily through each other and through other objects, and can penetrate the sea and the seeming solidity of the earth, merely by converting their frequency rate as the situation may demand.

As to the information contained in the foregoing paragraphs, I have only the following explanation to offer:

A. It comes through the deep-trance mediumship of a well-known medium, Mark Probert. The communicator in this instance is one Raymond Natalli, an astronomer and physicist contemporary with Shakespeare. Identities can never be conclusively 'proven', but they are comparitively unimportant. All that matters is the content of the communication.

B. I would not for a moment ask anyone to accept anything on the 'authority' of supernormal sources. I do respectfully ask that useful information should not be disregarded because of personal prejudice and hasty generalizations concerning 'psychism' or spiritism.

C. For 5 to 10 hours a week, for 7 - 8 years, I listened to the Probert controls and talked with them. They claim to be, and appear to be excarnate humans and fully integrated personalities. They have conducted themselves as honorable persons of good will. They are highly intelligent and widely informed, and have discussed a wide range of cultural and scientific subjects. They have had the respectful attention of scholars, scientists, and technicians and have engaged in many discussions with them.

D. It was these controls who gave us, in the fall of 1946, the first (and best and only) interpretation of the aeroforms. -- They make no claim to omniscience but warn us against such a claim from <u>any</u> source.

E. They are not Etherians, but normal humans from various astral levels who possess knowledge superior to our own - and desire to share it with us.

Since the combined knowledge of our own time - our science, religion, and philosophy - has as yet no worthwhile interpretation of the phenomena of the aeroforms, it might conceivably be the part of wisdom (and common sense) at least to listen to these would-be friends from the 'other side' - of course with all due reservations, suspicions, and face-saving provisos - and to put their offered knowledge to the test of study and practical application.

(I think our Associates, for whom this journal is published, are aware that I hold no brief for spiritualism as a religious 'movement' (and neither do the controls referred to); but I regard survival and communication as factual, as being inevitable and near-at-hand social acceptances, and as opening up immense resources of knowledge when properly utilized. Beyond this, 'each to his own place on his own path'. Vox clamantis non sum.)* m.l.

*Our Brochure 1-1-6 and other informational material relative to the aeroforms may be had from BSR Headquarters on request.

HOW FAST IS "FASTEST"?

If the speed of light is, as Einstein contended, a maximum and a constant for the universe, then an 'ether-ship' or any other object which attained this speed would have no dimensions, but an 'infinite' mass. If this is correct, it is obvious that any object or being attempting to 'cross' interstellar spaces would be held to a speed much below that of light. Since such distances are computed in light-years, the <u>time</u> required for such transit might run into centuries.

The scientifiction writers who love to dart about the stellar immensities with the joyous abandon of junebugs never openly admit that they are colliding with Professor Einstein's mathematics - in addition to the meteorites, bolides or what-have-you.

The distance from our system to Arcturus, for example, is said to be about 32.6 light years - and a light-year is about 182,000 x 60 x 60 x 24 x 365 miles. Give your Sunday-supplement aeronaut even a third of the light-speed and see how long his trip would take him. On behalf of the science-fiction addicts at any rate, some way must be found to wiggle out of this.

But according to our various planetary visitors, who get here in no time at all even from "beyond the galaxies", this wiggle or wriggle is a simple matter. They just don't believe in Einstein - at least when he says that the 'speed of light' is a maximum. They are aware that to 'be somewhere' - in some given place - means to be 'tuned in' on the frequencies of that place. When you tune-in or tune out you respond to a different environment - as 'any fool can plainly see' - to quote Al Capps. Also, 'you are where your consciousness is' - if you'll pardon the stale metaphysics.

So, what these etheric people are really doing, is not discrediting Einstein, but making a masterly detour. They're not talking about <u>mot</u>-<u>ion</u> at all, nor about <u>transit</u> of space. They're talking about being <u>here</u> and then being <u>there</u>.

And this seems to be the place to mention that there is no world-wide or science-wide agreement about the speed of light being a maximum. There is, in fact, what seems to be good evidence that radiesthetic energy is far 'faster'. We got into this little essay on account of what lately appeared in the <u>Metaphysical Digest</u> (Vol. iii, No. 2); and here it is:

"The implications are vital. Once again we have found that, contrary to expectations, we have an effect that influences light, but is not light in the ordinary scientific sense. The speed of radiesthetic energy assessed by comparitive methods, came out at some 200,000 times that of normal light ... Does not radiesthetic energy, psychic energy, thought energy, all transcend space-time as we know it by purely physical methods?"

In his book called <u>Space Travel</u>, Harold Goodwin remarks: "The Einsteinian conclusions are <u>not entirely</u> a matter of pure theory. When atomic particles are accelerated in the cyclotron, they do gain mass. Wouldn't it be odd if one of them some day <u>exceeded</u> the speed of light?"

Yes, indeed, Mr. Goodwin - but the world seems to be full of very "odd" happenings.

Mr. Goodwin then goes on to remark that: "The constancy of the speed of light has been challenged recently. Some researchers have found cyclic changes within 14 miles per second and there seem to be daily variations. An European scientist who has studied the subject for over a quarter of a century, M. de Bray, says that the alleged constancy of light is unsupported by observation. Physicists generally do not accept this point of view. They feel that the variations are due to factors other than changes in the velocity of light itself. If there should be variations, however, a main prop to relativity becomes as dead as the ether - which most scientists also defended."

Too bad that Mr. Goodwin* had to drag in that alleged demise of the ether 'theory' - since one could fill half this page with names of physicists who do not agree with him, and do agree with "it" -- subject, of course, to careful definition of the word <u>ether</u> and its derivatives.

However, Mr. Goodwin appears to approve of the concept of a space warp, which is said to change the geometry of the gravitational fields between celestial bodies. This would change the coordinates (position) of an object (say, a space-ship) and apparently avoids the idea of motion or transit, at least in 'occupied' space. So, it may be that the operations of etherian physicists will eventually be approved of by 'earthian' scientists also - which will be a great relief to all concerned.

I think I have said enough here, even in our school-boyish simplicity, to suggest that the concept of <u>emergence</u>, and of conversion of energy-frequencies in connection with the extraordinary phenomena of the aeroforms, is quite capable of serious scientific defense, even by 'earthian' physicists. A few well-chosen words from Bertrand Russell may give food for meditation:

"It may be found that the ether is, after all, what is fundamental, and that electrons and hydrogen nuclei are merely states of strain in the ether. . .

*(Ref. to Goodwin): The Science Book of Space Travel: Cardinal Edition of Pocket Books, Inc., N.Y., 1955.

"It is possible that an electron is a kind of disturbance in the ether, most intense at one spot. . . It is equally possible that a hydrogen nucleus may be explained in a similar way. . ."

Referring to the explanation we offer, that there is no 'crossing of space' measured in light years, by the aeroforms, Russell remarks that the process by which an electron changes its orbit is inexplicable since it happens instantaneously, contrary to all known physical laws. "Perhaps" - he says - "there is NO intervening space..."

In like manner the ether ships emerge from one frequency into another, and thereby appear in a different place. There is no "empty space" to cross, and hence no time required for the transit.

A brilliant brochure (60 pgs.) in support of the existence of the Ether, is The Ether and its Vortices, by physicist Carl F. Krafft. Annandale, Va. - 1955.

Eddington, as is well known, says emphatically that we cannot dispense with the ether, and that in trying to do so we have to attribute properties to the interspaces and represent them by a 'host of symbols'. The phrase 'empty space' is meaningless and the old problem of 'action at a distance' is still unconquered.

As to space, which is bound up with time, it is not an objective entity at all, but a concept based on the idea of geometrical points. But it is used by writers in a half-dozen senses and in no-sense and nonsense, always without attempt at definition. Here, once again, discretion is the better part.

**All quotes from Russell are from The ABC of Atoms.

THE LAYMAN AT LARGE

The word density, as has repeatedly been pointed out, is used in several different ways by physicists. The present comment is narrowly restricted to the current text-book definition - that density is determined by the quantity of matter per unit volume. If the quantity of matter within a given volume is increased while the volume remains constant, the density (mass, weight) is said to be increased.

Let us assume that we have (say) a cube of brick 10 cm on a side, and that this cube is completely enclosed in a tight container of the same exact interior dimensions. Let us suppose that means be supplied by application of intense heat to vaporize this brick cube while the container remains intact.

The vaporized cube or its container, obviously contains the same amount of matter as did the cube while in its solid form; hence D will be the same (under our definition of D). But we are now dealing with a gas, with a release of kinetic energy, with a different vibratory rate, etc.

If the vaporized substance were allowed to escape from its container, it would expand and be dissipated; but we are dealing with a constant volume, 1000 cu. cm. The vaporized cube is now invisible and intangible. But the wide atomic and molecular spaces within the solid brick allow plenty of 'room' or 'unoccupied' space so that, under pressure, a very large number of other vaporized cubes could be forced into the same cubic space. The density of the cube would then be greatly increased (more matter in the same over-all volume).

We would then have an invisible and intangible cube of far greater density than the original solid cube.

If we _imagine_ certain cohesive forces at work which would confine even the vaporized cube(s) to the original 1000 cu. cm. volume, without any container, there would exist in space a cube of enormous density which our senses would not detect.

Let us assume (what is indeed widely believed) that every so-called solid object has its "etheric double" or duplicate in etheric matter. It is also believed that such a "double" continues as an existent in its own right, even after the destruction of its 'solid' counterpart, may even be discerned (ESP) and/or detected by means employed in radiesthesia. In such case the double must persist by means of its own cohesive forces, (whereas a thought-form presumably depends on projected energy from some mental source).

An inference of some importance is, that just as the vaporized cube(s) are still wholly material and also may be much more dense than the original cube; so the etheric doubles may also be material and of higher density than their original objects. The analogy is incomplete in that the vaporized cube(s) will not maintain the original volume unless held by a container. The object of the analogy is to make obvious that etheric (and other) objects may be of very high density while remaining invisible, intangible, and wholly material.

The Etheric or "4-D" Interpretation of the Aeroforms - A Synopsis

The following paragraphs are intended as the shortest possible synopsis of the factors involved in this interpretation. The supporting data and reasoning are extensive and can be found in the various publications of the Borderland Research Associates.

(1) The aeroforms (flying discs, "saucers", and mutants or indescripts) are best understood with respect to their origin and nature as being EMERGENTS: that is, they emerge onto our plane of perception from a space time frame of reference which is different from ours. This process may also be described as a conversion of energy and a change of vibratory rates.

(2) That this is so, is obviously suggested by the phenomena themselves; since physical matter, as we know it, could not withstand the speed, temperature, and strain imposed by the observed operations of the discs and other forms. This does not conflict with the apparent composition of the 'landed ' discs.

(3) When the energy conversion mentioned in (1), sup., takes place, the aeroform becomes visible and tangible. It appears to be and definitely is what we call solid substance, and so remains until the vibratory rate is again converted. The "steel" of the landed disc is an etheric steel and its copper is etheric copper - since the prototypes of all our metals exist in etheric matter; nevertheless chemical analysis has shown certain radical differences. The conversion process amounts to materialization and dematerialization ("mat and demat"). "Demat" on our plane of perception would be "mat" for any consciousness functioning on the etheric level, and vice versa.

(4) Just as there is a spectrum of sound and of color (ending in sounds we cannot hear and colors we cannot see), so there is also a spectrum of tangibility, ending in forms of matter which are too dense to be touched. The ordinary matter of our plane is a rarefaction, and the interspaces between the nucleus and the electrons are relatively enormous. The extremely dense matter of the ethers passes through earth substance freely, and almost without friction. But if the vibratory rate of an etheric object is slowed down, it becomes less dense and enters our field of perception.

(5) With reference to our use of the word density: this word is used in different senses by physicists and demands definition, for which we cannot here take space.

(6) Etheric matter on account of its density is subject to the play of many subtle forces, including the energic activity of thought. Any form or object of which the mind can conceive can be brought into existence by mental action, and controlled by the same means. Etheric objects are in every way as "real" as those of our own world. And there

is abundant experimental evidence for the control of "mind over matter" on our own plane of perception.

(7) The foregoing paragraph applies also to the bodies of Etherian people. Our own bodies are truly made by our minds; we identify ourselves with them and control them. The Etherian makes his own body in a somewhat similar way, but quickly and easily, and makes it in any size and form he chooses. By the same principle, he can produce the form of a sphere, a cylinder, a cube, a disc or 'saucer' - and any desired vibrations of color and sound.

(8) Whether the Etherian people are "human" or not, depends entirely on one's definition of the word human. So far as we know, they are not excarnate humans and have not lived on our planet, though often visiting it. It is a cardinal mistake to assume that their bodies, and the other ships created by them are necessarily the same as we have seen them, when they withdraw to their own planes of existence. It is a cardinal mistake to assume that they are all of the same kind and 'race', or of the same moral character and evolutionary development.

(9) The 'vehicle' of an Etherian (whether his body or his 'ship') is thus essentially a thought-form (as our own bodies are also) - and a thought-form can be 'positioned' anywhere. The problems of space travel as we conceive them, do not exist for him - as implied by paragraph (1) above. By altering his vibratory rates the Disc Etherian penetrates our seas and the substance of our globe as easily as he does our atmosphere. All the aeroforms pass through each other (on occasion), and through our dwellings at will, and are (and probably always have been) invisibly present in varying numbers.

(10) The Etherians themselves (or entities purporting to be such) have given the following account:- -- That the first step in constructing the huge space craft ("mother ships" and other) is to isolate a cube of space (or ether) to the required vibration frequency. This etheric substance is then given the desired form, and the proper equipment is placed within it, according to its proposed station and operation . . . This work is done mainly by mental means: The Etherians make use of machines and apparatus, but these also are etheric constructs.

(11) When the'ship'is completed, it is placed by mental means ('teleportation') in any desired location (as, say, in the vicinity of our earth). So far, neither the ship nor any of these operations would be visible to us. But, if the frequency of the etheric matter is then converted to other specific rates, the ship will (or may) become visible and tangible to our senses. But there is NO "crossing of space" involved at any time. There is simply a change of location - and this is equivalent to a change of frequency or a conversion of vibratory rates.

(12) This last principle cannot be reiterated too often. It is basic to any understanding of the whole mass of the aeroform phenomena.

(13) These huge craft (to call them such) may be miles in dimension, or even of planetary size - hence the feasability of an 'evacuation of the planet' if necessary. Under what conditions these huge objects, hanging hundreds of miles overhead, are converted to a frequency rate perceptible to us, is, of course, unknown. But discs and other forms, discharged by mother ships, are obviously so converted, in order to operate under gravitational and magnetic conditions peculiar to our planet. Or, it may be a part of the over-all plan that these objects be made visible and tangible to us, as part of the education of the earth people.

(14) Recurring to the concept of "emergence", it may be helpful to quote the following illustration:
Suppose we have a series of concentric balls, one within another like the "Chinese eggs". Call the central ball, No. 1, and the others Nos. 2 - 3 - 4 etc. For any given point on, say, the 6th. ball, there will be a corresponding spot on both the inside and the outside of ball No. 5 and of ball No. 7 - and so on all the other balls also. Consider that each ball has its own vibration rate. Then if you wish to move any object on (say) ball 6 and place it on ball 5 or 7, you simply change its vibration rate accordingly. The object then will be located in a new place. It will not have to "pass over" any intervening space - it simply comes into existence in a new location. A change of frequency is equivalent to a change of location.

(15) Such a statement as "I am here" means simply that I am "tuned in" to objects, sounds and colors of my surroundings. If this receptivity were altered so that "I tuned out", the environment would disappear, but would be replaced by a different one unless the change destroyed me. This would be a space-time operation and a change of location without transit of space.

(16) Contemporary distrust of the concept of the other is unjustified and must be left to physicists who do not seem sufficiently familiar with the literature of their own subject.

(17) So far (August 1955) the whole mass of material on aeroforms, with some tentative exceptions, has not produced an over-all interpretation which is at once intelligible science and sound metaphysics. Yet the interpretation reported by us and here summarized is steadily gaining ground, and we bespeak its thoughtful consideration on its own merits. It will be expanded and altered in details but it is basically correct.

** ** ** ** **

EXCERPTS FROM LETTER
                ROLF TELANO to Meade Layne

. . . "Regarding the matter of forthcoming events, there is probably no
reason why an advanced group such as the BSRA could not know the truth.
In fact, it might be helpful if they did, since it would lead them to
make any necessary mental preparations.

First, I should like to make it clear that my people are not "Gods"
or any other sort of supernatural beings. They do live on a higher vibratory plane. They have advanced considerably above the people of this
planet in both material and mental sciences. They do have a very long
life span as compared to that of earthlings, and so have time to acquire
a considerable amount of knowledge in one 'incarnation'. I like to
think that, on the average, they have risen somewhat higher than the
earthlings in morals, ethics, and spiritual development. However, this
is not invariably true on an individual basis, for some of them are evil.
In brief, their mental processes and emotional reactions are quite
'human', and are, therefore, subject to all human error.

Secondly, they disclaim any ability to truly foretell events in the
usual and mystical sense of the word. What they do is to take as many
facts as they can obtain, analyze them in the light of history and experience, and project them forward to discover what is the most probable
sequence of events. They not only have very great mental abilities themselves, but can also tune in to the Cosmic Mind for information, if desired. Thus the probability of their analysis is usually very high.
There may be only one chance in a million that things will not be as
they say, but there is still that chance, and it is therefore still only
the most probable forecast, and not true prophecy.

Keeping these limitations in mind, I can pass along the forecast
that some great catastrophe is likely to take place very soon. They cannot say just how soon nor exactly how severe. Both of these depend upon
several variables. However, it will be relatively soon, and relatively
severe in loss of life and property. It will consist for the most part
of a series of 'natural calamities' - earthquakes, floods, etc. They will
be, however, 'man -made' in a basic sense. That is, both the atomic experiments and certain mental attitudes of the peoples are causing ether-
eal stresses which will have this result. The variable factors consist
of what governments and peoples do in the future. IF they should cease
their release of atomic energy, and IF the masses of the people should
correct the pattern of their thinking, then these events would be delayed and made less severe. There is no evidence at present that either
of these things will happen.

The reason for not revealing these facts to the public at large is
that, from a practical point of view, there is nothing they can do to

avoid the end result. They apparently are doomed, but it would be cruel
to tell them so. Very few would believe in any event, but those who did
believe would die daily from then on. If they are allowed to remain in
ignorance of their fate, they will go about their usual and ordinary oc-
cupations, and their passing will be relatively brief and with the mini-
mum amount of terror. B.S.R. Associates, on the other hand, have more
realization of the fact that the act of passing from this plane is not
tragic or important in itself. The reasons and circumstances may be
important, but not the act per se.

It might be well for even B.S.R.Associates to fix more firmly in
their minds that life is a continuing thing. It cannot be destroyed,
only transformed to some other plane. Thus one does not really lose
his 'life'. He merely loses his material body, and this is a relatively
unimportant and transitory thing. What happens to it is important only
in a few exceptional circumstances. What happens to the real person who
is inhabiting that body at the moment is very important. There are often
times when it is better to lose the mortal body, if the real immortal
inner self would be degraded by the circumstances of retaining it.

In the times of great stress which seem to lie ahead, it will often
come to pass that a man must lose his "life" in order to gain his life.

January 23, 1956   Fraternally --- R. T. *

* R. T. is an engineer by profession and a resident of the
State of Ohio.

The above was issued as Personal Bulletin No. 6, to BSR Associates,
February 1956.

** ** ** ** **

THE IDEALISTIC POINT OF VIEW

(One of the most profound and brilliant philosophers of modern times was George Berkeley, Bishop of Cloyne, 1685 - 1753. There is much in common between his metaphysics and the 'all-consciousness' school of Oriental philosophy. The following exposition is selected from Weber; Hist. Philos., 393 ff.)

Just as color, smell and taste exist only for the person perceiving them, so extension, form and motion exist only in a mind that perceives them. Take away the perceiving subject and you take away the sensible world. Existence consists in perceiving or being perceived. That which is not perceived and does not perceive does not exist. Objects do not exist apart from the subjects perceiving them.. . . There is no real difference between things and our ideas of them. The word sensible thing and idea are synonymous.

In so far as mind perceives ideas (things) it produces things. The ideas are things themselves. But since all objects do not depend on one's will for their being perceived, there must be some other will that produces them (God). Laws of nature are the set rules by which the Great Mind produces in us the ideas (objects) of sense.

There is no material substratum of "matter" which supports the various qualities which our senses report to us. But there is a plurality of minds, and that which is not perceived by one mind may be maintained in existence by other minds or the Great Mind.

Men assume the objective and independent existence of matter, because they feel that they are not the authors of their own sensations, and hence refer their origin to matter instead of to the creative Mind, because the course of Nature seems regular, yet the occurrence of a 'miracle' often disturbs them in this contradictory notion.

"This in my opinion" (says Weber) "is the only metaphysic that may be successfully opposed to materialism, overcomes the dualism of substances and satisfies the philosophic demand for unity."

The control Natalli, being asked: How does a room look when nobody sees it? replied in effect: The opposite of existence is latency. The unperceived object persists as an energy form, or as a potentiality in the sea of cosmic being. If one enters the room and "sees" its objects, his mind is evoking them according to the natural laws of its action. The thing-in-itself does not exist unless the words mean the energy which maintains and evokes the forms. Mind alone exists, and time, space, and causation cannot exist apart from mind.

It is because of these facts that whenever Science ventures upon a pronouncement on the 'final nature' of anything, it becomes hopelessly involved with metaphysics. The separation of the two is a dichotomy, an artifical and temporary device in an effort to think an unintelligible world.

ml

WHAT DO YOU MEAN - SPACE?

Nothing is more desperately needed just now, than a little attention to elementary semantics - simply to the definition of words. Let us explore very superficially, the meaning of a single term - SPACE - even at the risk of being deadly dull.

SPACE in the philosophy of Aristotle means "the container of all objects". If no objects, no container. In a Void without objects, Space could not exist. In a void with one object only - say, a single point, position would not exist.

In Kantian metaphysics, Space, like time and causation, is a form of mind action, or consciousness. Our minds are so made that we are aware of the world today only as it exists in Space and Time.

In modern mathematics, Space is a name for certain abstract groups or sets. It is not an objective entity. It is a concept, and as such is bound up with another idea, that of Time. All objects exist in three dimensions, and also in Time. This gives us the 4-dimensional universe called the omniverse. Minkowski opened up this line of thought, and Einstein incorporated both the special and general theories of relativity.

This Space-Time concept is based on the idea of geometrical points. A geometrical point has position only, does not have duration. If it is given duration it will produce a geometrical line. Space-Time is a term for the general structure of world events and objects -- for "4-D" events. The Omniverse cannot move or change, but we can think of change and motion, if Space and Time are regarded separately. No absolute separation is possible, but in a coordinate system we can think of them that way.

Space-Time is regarded somewhat differently by such thinkers as S. Alexander and C.L. Morgan, under the concept of Emergent Evolution. According to this, Space-Time is the universal matrix of matter, life, mind and even of Deity. "God" is an Emergent.

On a somewhat mystic level, Space is sometimes described as "that form of reality which is not perceived by our senses".
Mathematicians cannot get along without Space - nor with it. They assign symbols and properties to it, but cannot treat it as an existent, nor recognize that it equates with the ether. The term "empty space" is meaningless -- and so is the statement that the ether "fills space." Russell's definition of an electron, as " a wave of probability with nothing to wave in" shows the metaphysical poverty of such thinking -- brilliant as its achievements may otherwise be. It seems certain that the ether will once again be accepted as the basic cosmic entity. As to whether or not the ether (or space, or ether-space) is material, depends on your definition of matter. Always ask for definitions. Always be sure you have one if you are asked.

THE PHILOSOPHY OF THE COMMUNICATORS

(Mediumship of Mark Probert)

(Philosophical comments by the Communicators at Mark Probert Seances
are widely scattered through some hundreds of pages of memoranda and reports, and we cannot here present the various questions asked, or the
verbatim replies. The interest in this material, however, justifies one
or two pages of Clips & Quotes in this issue, with brief continuing sec-
tions in several issues to come. For topics to be covered, see note at
end of this article.)

The Continuum:

Question: Is there such a thing as a continuum in Nature - any-
which is homogenous, not particulate, or corresponding to the older of
the ether?

Answer: This is not a yes-or-no question; it has what logicians
call an excluded middle. It depends on what you mean by thing. There
is no homogenous substance or stuff, but there are various ethers of
varying degrees of fineness, and of varying frequency rates.

Remember that ether is a term for an existent in space. Now Space
as a projected idea, as some-thing imagined to exist by itself, cannot
be a continuum, because the mind cannot produce such a concept without
falling into contradiction. But the consciousness which produces the
space idea is itself a kind of continuum, because it lives in an eternal now and an eternal here. Anything existing in time and space has to
be discrete, made up of parts, such as atoms of matter and instants of
time and points of space. But consciousness does not exist in space
and time.
Space and time are "in" the consciousness, or are the modes of its
functioning. What we have, and are, is awareness in a timeless present,
so to speak. I mean, consciousness is a timeless activity or 'pure' activity.
In this I am speaking of separate individual minds, or persons or
individuals. We can trace all phenomena of the sense world back to the
functioning of individual minds. Everything you know about an object,
all of its qualities, reduces to states or activity of consciousness or
awareness. But we are also aware that there is a plural number of minds.
"A" is aware that "B" exists; and "B" is aware of "A", and so on. "A" is
creating his own space-time world, and "B" is creating his. Also, these
two spearate mind-created worlds have much in common, in the form of
what you call the "same" experiences at the "same" time, very often.
This last fact usually leads the philosopher to postulate something
in addition to individual minds. A postulate is a necessary assumption.

He can't think the universe without this postulate (nor with it either, perhaps). If you try to think of the Absolute, or God as a First Cause, you are thinking in terms of time and causation, and these are functions or forms of your own mind. And a "first cause" is something which has no cause itself, and this destroys the whole principle of causation or reasoning by which you are working. The reason always commits suicide when it looks for a first explanation or first cause - and yet it cannot get along without one. All the reason can do, really, is to operate in the field of manifestation, and neither to affirm nor deny the Absolute. ... Of course, when you speak of emotions and instinct and religious faith you are in another field of discourse.

Going back to the form of your first question, remember that the world of your physical senses, of phenomena, of sense impressions, is a world which is projected by or perhaps through your individual minds. Your minds are so made that the external world, as you call it, is subject to time and space and causation. And so matter and energy also has to be discrete or particulate. And the mind finds in itself the laws which obtain in this mind-made world. It is the mind discovering itself. That is what science is. Nature is always Nature-as-known-to-consciousness. There is nothing else to appeal to. You cannot say anything at all about Nature-in-itself, but only about nature as perceived by you. Intuition and instinct will give you certain experiences, but now we are talking about reason and logic and the world of sense perception.

The Thing-in-Itself (Ding-an-Sich):

The question as to whether the thing-in-itself exists is like the question about the continuum. It is not a yes-or-no question as it stands.

Your mind is a centralized or focalized activity. It forms ideas and images - say, the image of a cube. That energy or power that takes the cube form might be called the cube-in-itself. You don't need to say it is your own mind making the cube; but the cosmic energy or life is functioning through your center and making it. Of course, it is silly to talk as if there is some kind of 'material stuff' put 'out there' in space to make a cube. That is not philosophy but only childishness. Stuff and shape and distance and form are things created by mind - like time and space and causation. The cube-in-itself is the creative force which produces the cube-form, and that force is of a mental order. All energy is of this same type in the last analysis.

* ** ** ** ** **

Other subjects discussed by the Controls include CHANGE -- THE SUB-CONSCIOUS -- RESPONSIBILITY -- THE HIGH SELF -- MEDITATION AND FEAR; and some of these will be summarized in CQC-E-5. Its publication here is somewhat experimental and we would like to hear the opinions of our readers.

ml

(from CQC E-4, Aug. 15,1955)

THE NEGATIVE PROTON *

by   C. F. KRAFFT.

This recently discovered sub-atomic particle has about the same mass as the proton, but carries a negative electric charge instead of a positive charge, and is about twice the size of the proton. Under the prevailing doctrines of theoretical physics, such a particle cannot be accounted for. If its size is determined by its mass, as most physicists seem to think, then it should be of about the same size as the proton and not twice the size thereof. On the other hand, if it were a composite structure formed of one proton and two electrons, then its size would be over three times the size of the proton. Neither can it be a combination of a neutron and an electron because neutrons have no affinity for electrons.

On page 36 of my book, The Ether and its Vortices, published long before the negatron was discovered experimentally, I have shown two of these negatrons as constituent parts of the carbon atom; and it will be observed that my negatron does have a size just about twice the size of the proton. No doubt the physics profession will eventually find some "explanation" for the negatron, but the successful prediction of an unexpected fact is more convincing than any amount of wisdom after the fact.

- end -

The foregoing memorandum from physicist C. F. Krafft gives indirect support to the Ether Vortex Theory developed by him in his brochure The Ether and its Vortices (66 pgs.) and should be of much interest not only to many BSR Associates but to the entire physics profession. The brochure is obtainable from most university and public libraries, or in request from the author, at the nominal price of $1.00. Address C.F. Krafft, Route 2, Box 687, Annandale, Virginia.

ml

. (* reprinted from C.Q.C. - F 3, Mar.15,1956)

A MEMO FROM NATALLI:

The SPACE CRAFT will not run on magnetic propulsion beyond the ionosphere. The ionosphere would destroy any magnetic sink between the craft and the earth. Beyond that limit they operate on solar energy.

There is almost no effect of the earth's magnetic field beyond the ionosphere. The magnetic field will change according to the density of the nearest body. The craft will depend almost entirely on the solar energy. The colors noted about these craft are not due to temperature changes, but to electronic changes.

No earth metal could stand such heat changes without becoming very brittle. It is the play of electrons produced by the solar radiation on the body of the craft and produces conditions similar to those that cause the Aurora Borealis.

-- Dictated by the Natalli control, Nov.3,1954

CONCERNING THE MARK PROBERT MEDIUMSHIP

Mark Probert was born in Bayonne, New Jersey, in 1907, and attended the grammar school there through the sixth grade. He went to sea in the merchant marine for two years, and afterward came to California, where he was a dancer and entertainer for a time, and held various 'odd jobs'. He developed a talent for portrait painting (without any instruction) and still prefers that to any other occupation. There was a touch of psychism in his family, and he himself had many odd experiences while still a boy.

The more systematic development of his mediumship began in 1945-46, when a series of sittings were held at his home in San Diego. They were marked at first by a remarkable xenoglossy, or 'gift of tongues', and for some weeks it was difficult to get any communications in English. Soon, however, the first of the present Controls took charge, and there has been a steady improvement in the receptivity - and in the physical health - of the medium. The quality of the 'messages' received has been uniformly high - concerned for the most part with questions in science, philosophy, metaphysics and cultural subjects generally. No religionist or cultist approach is involved, nor will the controls permit it.

All the meetings are held in full light and no 'physical phenomena' occur. Mark simply 'goes to sleep' and the various Controls talk through him. They are fully integrated personalities, highly informed, and anxious to serve their friends on this side in every possible way. The communications are now widely known in the Western States, and thousands of pages of reports and transcripts of them have been made available in mimeographed form. The Director and Associates of the Borderland Sciences have cooperated in all this, so far as their limited resources have permitted. We consider Mark Probert to be one of the most remarkable deep-trance mediums now living, and that knowledge of the highest importance has become available through his powers.

M. L.

E & D: The Planetary Logos — undifferentiated.
        The Universal Mind.

F: The Great Depths, or Sea Trenches (5 to 6 miles).
    "F" is also the summits of the mountains of
    Etheria — — The Etheric penetrates to "E" but
    for practical purposes may be considered as
    ending at "F".

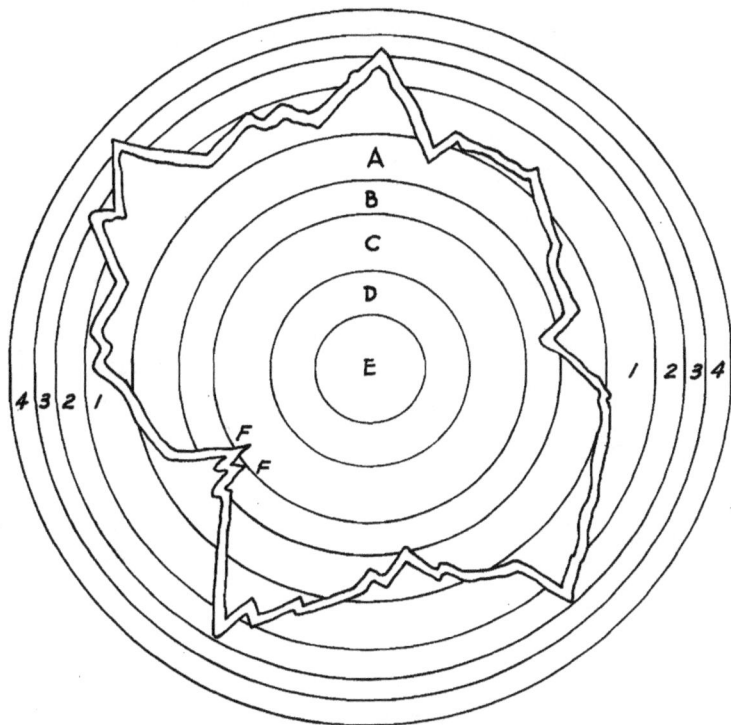

A,B,C,D,E are the traditional divisions of the "Inner
Planes". The jagged lines are the mountains of our
globe, rising into the etheric and descending into A,
B & C. The dimensions of the Etheric circles should
be much larger.

    The greatest heights of the etheric mountains
are the deepest parts of our seas.

    This chart, in more detailed and exact form was
given to G. K. by Etherian Guides & Instructors.

www.ingramcontent.com/pod-product-compliance
Lightning Source LLC
La Vergne TN
LVHW091204080426
835509LV00006B/825